The Balkans, nationalism and imperialism

The Balkans, nationalism and imperialism

Edited by Lindsey German

BOOKMARKS

London, Chicago and Sydney

The Balkans, Nationalism and Imperialism – Edited by Lindsey German
First published 1999
Bookmarks Publications Ltd, c/o 1 Bloomsbury Street, London WC1B 3QE, England
Bookmarks, PO Box 16085, Chicago, Illinois 60616, USA
Bookmarks, PO Box A338, Sydney South, NSW 2000, Australia
Copyright © Bookmarks Publications Ltd

ISBN 1 898876 49 5 (Hardback)
ISBN 1 898876 50 9 (Paperback)

Printed by Larkham Printing and Publishing
Cover by Sherborne Design

Bookmarks Publications Ltd is linked to an international grouping of socialist organisations:
- **Australia:** International Socialist Organisation, PO Box A338, Sydney South
- **Britain:** Socialist Workers Party, PO Box 82, London E3 3LH
- **Canada:** International Socialists, PO Box 339, Station E, Toronto, Ontario M6H 4E3
- **Cyprus:** Ergatiki Demokratia, PO Box 7280, Nicosia
- **Denmark:** Internationale Socialister, PO Box 5113, 8100 Aarhus C
- **Germany:** Linksruck, Postfach 304 183, 20359 Hamburg
- **Greece:** Socialistiko Ergatiko Komma, c/o Workers Solidarity, PO Box 8161, Athens 100 10
- **Holland:** Internationale Socialisten, PO Box 92025, 1090AA Amsterdam
- **Ireland:** Socialist Workers Party, PO Box 1648, Dublin 8
- **New Zealand:** Socialist Workers Organisation, PO Box 8851, Auckland
- **Norway:** Internasjonale Socialisterr, Postboks 9226 Grønland, 0134 Oslo
- **Poland:** Solidarność Socjalistyczna, PO Box 12, 01-900 Warszawa 118
- **Spain:** Socialismo Internacional, Apartado 563, 08080 Barcelona
- **United States:** International Socialist Organization, PO Box 16085, Chicago, Illinois 60616
- **Zimbabwe:** International Socialist Organisation, PO Box 6758, Harare

Contents

Bosnia

And after much talking, the bomb stood up and spoke:
Friends, I speak for civilisation and culture
I speak in the great tradition of standing up to fascism
I speak for the rights of small nations
Abyssinia, Czechoslovakia, Poland
I speak in the name of—
(here the bomb lowered his voice)
I speak in the name of the six million Jews

The room fell quiet
a roomful of our generals and leaders
all bearing emblems of peace and goodwill unto all men
all bearing fatigues and armour
blood-spattered from the battlefields
of Belfast, Port Stanley, Panama and Baghdad
all sweating and straining to keep control of their world disorder.

One leapt to his feet.
What can you do for us?
And the bomb replied
I can fly from the sky and find out your enemy
I can seek the culprit
pinpoint the armaments that deal out such pain and misery
and,
like honey on fresh bread,
I can spread peace and comfort to all.

Then our leaders spoke in agreement:
we can select an enemy
we can choose a culprit
we can set your sights
we can show the world
that we can solve problems
we can win respect
we can keep power
we can keep power
we can keep power

Not so fast gentlemen, said the bomb
I am but one.
Before sending me on my mission
you must make many more like me.

No problem
bellowed back our leaders,
each fresh from downsizing a hospital
from taking the slack out of pensions
from slimming down some meals on wheels
no problem
we can make bombs
we can make bombs
go, do your best, make peace.

And the bomb got up and left the room
and did what he has always done
whether it was in Guernica or Dresden
Hanoi or Baghdad
he found out, he sought, he pinpointed
someone driving a bus
someone bathing a wound
someone digging potatoes
someone scrubbing a floor.

And so it is that in the forests and mountains
victims become culprits
culprits become victims
culprits become victims
victims become culprits
and so it is that their generals and leaders
and our generals and leaders
send the starving victim-culprits
down to the shops to stand in queues
to buy guns and shells and tanks—
send them to clean each other off their farms and fields.

And all this time
their generals and leaders
and our generals and leaders
stroll on the lawns of international conference centres
explaining their position vis a vis the safe havens
yes, the safe havens,
not intending with that
to refer to their own skins
their own suits
and their own beds.

You generals and leaders in khaki, grey or light blue
you are not the solution
you are the problem
we will not choose between you
we will not say that one of you
cleanses more reasonably than another
that one of you brings peace in his briefcase or tank
we will not wave any of your flags
we will not sing any of your tunes
and we will not join your dance of death.

Michael Rosen, September 1995

Introduction

Lindsey German

Little over a decade ago it seemed inconceivable that there could be major war in Europe. Yet in 1999 we have lived through two and a half months of bombing in the Balkans. This is the latest stage in a series of Western interventions in the former Yugoslavia which have been continuing for over ten years. The human cost of the war has been devastating, and the consequences are likely to be further misery, division and devastation.

This book is a collection of writings which cover that period, and which try to explain why the events which happened took place, how they could have been stopped, and what the possible alternatives were to war and division. They are mainly from the monthly magazine *Socialist Review*, but also from the quarterly journal *International Socialism*. Both publications have always argued against Western intervention and the right wing regime of Slobodan Milosevic, as well as against the nationalist regimes elsewhere in the region.

The war has caused tensions and instability throughout the Balkans, which can easily lead to the increase in the human misery that we have already seen. The Western powers will no doubt claim that there is a long history of ethnic division, and that the only humanitarian solution is to separate these people off into areas guarded by outside peace-keepers so that future conflicts cannot arise. They also say that the plight of the area is all the fault of one man, Slobodan Milosevic, who they describe as the new Hitler. This conveniently expunges all blame from the Western powers, which are not in any sense a neutral outside force. Their intervention has, by any criterion, made the situation much worse. Indeed, it is impossible to understand the recent history of the Balkans without recognising that successive Western interventions have exacerbated many of the problems there.

Yugoslavia can be seen as the most extreme example of the collapse of Communism which took place across the whole of Eastern Europe and the Soviet Union in the late 1980s. The failure of the nationalised command economies in these countries to compete with an increasingly internationalised Western capitalism led to a series of economic and political crises in the former Eastern bloc, of which Yugoslavia's was the most dramatic. Its turn to the West for loans further exacerbated this crisis. In 1983 the IMF was called in, and in the same year food rationing was introduced. By 1987 Yugoslav debt to the West stood at $20 billion and it had the highest unemployment rate in Europe. Workers responded to IMF inspired attacks on their living standards, which would have meant wage cuts of between 10 and 50 percent, with a wave of strikes. By 1988 inflation was at 150 percent, with 15 percent unemployment. Workers were in regular protests and strikes, leading to splits inside the ruling Communist Party bureaucracy. It was in the late 1980s that Milosevic, then the Communist Party boss in Serbia, first played the nationalist card. Serbian nationalists called for a tightening up of the federation and a clampdown in Kosovo. Milosevic addressed a mass rally in Belgrade towards the end of 1988 and demanded that the then autonomous provinces of Kosovo and Vojvodina be incorporated into Serbia. In this way he sought to deflect the class anger which many workers in Serbia and elsewhere in Yugoslavia felt against the bureaucrats who were wrecking their lives. The tragedy of the past decade has been the way in which national rather than class solutions have been taken up by sections of the population, backed by rulers who wanted to use it to build their popularity.

When in 1991 these tensions came to a head and the bureaucracies of the various Yugoslav republics, unable to resolve the crisis, began to abandon a centralised state in order to go their own way, the Western powers again played a decisive role in increasing tensions. Austria and Germany in particular encouraged the moves towards independence of the two richest regions, Slovenia and Croatia, even though this was almost certain to lead to war and ethnic cleansing. The British government was persuaded to back independence for Croatia by Germany in return for opt outs from the Maastricht treaty. When faced with the war which inevitably did come, first in Croatia and then spreading to Bosnia, the Western powers increasingly intervened. At first some of them saw the greatest stability in the region coming from trying to hold the state of Yugoslavia together, and therefore they were willing to back Milosevic's regime. But as this prospect became more and more untenable, they increasingly turned against Serbia and towards Croatia. US and NATO backing for Croatia in the Bosnian war led to the decisive defeat by Croatia of the Bosnian Serbs and the murderous ethnic cleansing of 200,000 Serbs from the Krajina region—many of whom then settled in Kosovo.

The Dayton agreement in 1995, which was meant to bring peace to Bosnia, was created on the back of ethnic cleansing. Its result has been that Bosnia is now effectively a foreign protectorate to which very large numbers of refugees have not returned. Milosevic may now be called the new Hitler, but in 1995 he was the man that the West could do business with. Milosevic turned a blind eye to the ethnic cleansing of the Krajina; in turn, the Western powers specifically excluded Kosovo from Dayton, thus leaving unresolved the oppression of the Albanians and the problem of future autonomy or independence.

Today we see the brutal logic of this repeated intervention, as Western troops are now in what looks like very long term occupation of much of the Balkans. There will be 50,000 Western troops in Kosovo itself. But there are also troops in Bosnia, Albania and Macedonia. Croatia has a pro-Western army. The former Yugoslavia is surrounded by NATO members Greece, Turkey and Hungary. It is obvious that NATO has very different aims in the region than the humanitarian ones which it employed to win support for this war. The fact that a month before the bombing started three new states from the former Warsaw Pact (Hungary, Poland and the Czech Republic) were admitted to NATO membership and therefore into the pro-Western camp has been largely ignored. Similarly, the fact that five former Soviet Union states formed a pro-Western confederation known as GUUAM (Georgia, Ukraine, Uzbekhistan, Azerbaijan and Moldova), while its representatives attended NATO birthday celebrations in Washington during the war in April 1999, has met with little comment. Yet both facts point to the real reason for this war: NATO is trying to expand its influence to incorporate much of the former Eastern bloc and so be able to intervene in far more situations. The importance of the oil and gas pipelines round the Caspian Sea is one reason for this strategic expansion; another is the protection of Western investment in much of Eastern Europe.

There would, of course, have been very little support for the bombing of Serb civilians had the war been justified in terms of the self interest of Western governments and big business. Instead this was painted as a war for humanitarian aims and, crucially, was carried ideologically by two groups of people not normally associated with warmongering—

the former radicals and peace activists who now form the core of the Labour and social democratic governments around Europe, and their ideological mouthpieces in the liberal media who used left credentials in order to sell a brutal and indefensible war. The fact that Robin Cook, the British foreign secretary, and his German counterpart, Joschka Fischer, were both peace activists, and that Bill Clinton evaded the Vietnam draft, was used to claim that this was a just war, unlike the previous ones that these same people had opposed. Yet the reality was that the wars had not changed. Every war has been justified in humanitarian terms, from the First World War to Vietnam; it is only later that the truth about such wars comes out and the vast majority of people see them as wasteful and pointless. The increasing justification for continuing the bombing as war went on was that NATO could not afford to lose face. This showed that any humanitarian questions were of low priority to the warmongers. It was the politics of Cook and Fischer which had changed, not the fundamental nature of the war.

Labour has always supported imperialist war, from the First World War to Vietnam, but with Tony Blair there was a particular new hawkishness about his enthusiasm for the war and his attempts to paint Britain as the main protagonist—attempts which looked increasingly foolish, as the deal eventually reached was brokered essentially between Germany, Russia and the US. The full talents of the Blairite spin doctors were put to explaining the NATO case, and at one time Alastair Campbell—Blair's closest adviser and spin doctor—was reputedly spending half his week in Brussels advising NATO press spokesman James Shea. The pro-war coverage in papers such as the *Guardian* was astonishing: there was a high level of propaganda and censorship, and the anti-war movement or anti-war views were barely reported.

Because there are Labour and social democratic governments in many of the NATO countries, the war led to a split on the left. Well known left wingers such as Ken Livingstone and Daniel Cohn-Bendit came out as fervent supporters of the war, while many others supported the anti-war movement. This led to deep bitterness in the arguments, but also to divisions and splits inside the left parties. The German SPD and Greens were both deeply divided, and it was commonly agreed that any attempt by the 'Red-Green' coalition to introduce ground troops would have led to a huge government crisis and possibly its downfall. In Britain, Blair was able to keep the lid on dissent inside the Labour Party, refusing even a vote on the war in parliament. Most

Labour MPs did not speak out openly against the war, although the handful who did clearly reflected much greater unease among the Parliamentary Labour Party. Anecdotal evidence showed widespread opposition to the war among Labour Party members, especially many activists. However, the suppression of debate and democratic discussion inside Labour meant there were few channels for expression of this discontent.

As the Kosovan phase of the Balkan War ended, its consequences were likely to be grim. The US and the NATO powers hailed the settlement as a victory, although they never expected the war to be so long and so bloody. They were also split over which tactics to follow, with Germany, Italy and Greece especially under tremendous political pressure not to send in ground troops. The US was also unable to do so, given the legacy of the Vietnam War. But the occupation of Kosovo by the Western powers may make them more confident to intervene in other parts of the globe after this adventure, just as its bombing of Iraq before Christmas 1998 increased its confidence to attack Serbia. Socialists have a duty to oppose imperialist war because of the destruction its wreaks, and also because of the way it strengthens the imperial powers and the capitalist classes they represent. But we also need an analysis of a system which breeds war as the most deadly means of competition between different capitalist powers. It is only by developing such a view of capitalism as a whole and a proper explanation of imperialism that it is possible to understand the particular twists and turns involved in various military interventions and wars.

This collection of articles has stood the test of time. The analysis repeatedly argued in them has been vindicated. There have, of course, been changes in emphasis reflecting changes in the political situation. For example, we developed a critique of the Kosovo Liberation Army as it became apparent that it was being used as an arm of NATO intervention. We have constantly tried to explain imperialism and Western intervention through a concrete explanation of the Balkan situation at every stage. We have also consistently argued that it is wrong in the context of the Balkans to take the side of any particular nationality or power in the region. In effect the Western powers have taken sides, and this has led to more ethnic cleansing, to more partition and to seeing the very deep problems of the region simply in national or ethnic terms. This has played into the hands of the respective national rulers and has made the task of those who want a socialist, democratic or class solution in the area much harder.

The tragedy of the Balkans is that the ordinary working people of the different nationalities have much more in common than divides them, yet the attempts by many workers at various times to fight for a class solution has been subsumed by national division and war. There is no easy way of overcoming that in the immediate future as those living in Serbia and Kosovo face ruin and devastation around them. Yet the divisions between rulers and ruled which exist in every society will surface again, as we see who will be expected to pay the cost of this war, both in the Balkans and in the West. In such situations a growing number of the different peoples of the region can begin to look to solutions which unite them across ethnic divisions against their common class enemy. Socialists living in the belligerent countries of the West can contribute to this process by showing solidarity with their sisters and brothers in the Balkans and by opposing the bloody imperialism of their own rulers. They can also help by providing a proper analysis of why these events have taken place. This book is a small contribution to developing our understanding of the roots of the latest conflict and showing how by looking at the bigger picture we can begin to build an alternative.

June 1999

Chapter 1

The nightmare of the market

Mike Haynes

The importance of the Yugoslav case for socialists lies both in the fact that it was the first Eastern European economy to break away from Russian influence and the Stalinist economic model, and in the fact that today it is in deep and seemingly endless crisis. If the stagnation in the majority of the Comecon countries shows the failure of central planning, Yugoslavia represents no less the worst case scenario for those who would want to shift towards some kind of 'market socialism'.

Tito and the Yugoslav Communist Party came to power at the end of the Second World War. They headed a movement of mass popular resistance to the Nazis and their Yugoslav collaborators. This separated their experience from that of the other Eastern European countries, where the support for the Communist Parties was much weaker and the role of the Red Army correspondingly more pronounced. Tito had no need of compromise or conciliation with the old order, and could move immediately towards the implementation of the Stalinist model. This is what happened. Yugoslavia quickly reproduced the main features of the Russian system. The documents of the first five year plan alone were said to have weighed one and a half tons! But beneath the adherence to the Moscow line, conflict was brewing. Tito had already put himself forward as the protector of Yugoslavia as a nation. 'No matter how much each of us loves the land of socialism—the USSR—he can, in no case, love his country less, which is also developing socialism,' he said in this period. Tension had existed during the war over the amount of Russian aid to the partisans and the political line that came with it.[1] When pressure came after the war to tie Yugoslav development more closely to the needs of the USSR, Tito

First published in an extended version winter 1988

had the base at home to resist this. The dispute exploded into the open in June 1948 when the Cominform (set up as the successor to the defunct Third International) passed a resolution condemning Tito and Yugoslav policy. At first the reaction of the Yugoslav leadership was to intensify their Stalinist policies in the hope of winning their way back into the fold, but as the pitch of conflict grew they gradually began to differentiate themselves.[2] Pushing them further in this direction were the increasing economic difficulties of the country. In 1947, 48.3 percent of Yugoslav trade had been with Russia, Czechoslovakia and Hungary. In 1950, as a result of a Russian blockade, this was reduced to nearly zero. This, combined with the negative internal consequences of the Stalinist policies and the coincidence of bad harvests, meant that from 1947 to 1952 the economy grew at only 1 percent per year—half the rate of the despised 1930s and one third the rate of the 1920s.

This differentiation had an internal dimension in the form of the development of self management and a greater reliance on the market. Externally it also involved a greater involvement with the world market and the use of Western aid (a first US loan of $20 million was forthcoming in September 1949). At the same time Tito attempted to show his independence by sponsoring the development of the nonaligned movement in the late 1950s. All of these features made Yugoslavia appear an attractive alternative to the rest of Eastern Europe, and when growth developed at a rapid pace in the 1950s and 1960s the 'Yugoslav miracle' quickly generated an enthusiastic following.[3] Yugoslav propagandists and Western fellow travellers explained the achievements in terms of the stimulus given by the self management model. How miraculous the record was can be disputed, and it seems unlikely that self management offers much of an explanation for performance—in the boom many different types of economy all grew very fast.[4] But these difficulties were rarely raised in a period when Yugoslavia, and indeed Tito himself, received endorsement from a wide range of sources in the West.

This is not to say that some problems were not recognised. Growth was subject to considerable cyclical instability. Unlike Eastern Europe, where the same cycles could also be found, Yugoslav commentators were quite open about the problem. Horvat devoted a pioneering study to showing how:

> ...indices of economic movements, corrected for seasonal fluctuations, reveal the existence of business cycles in Yugoslavia... Because of the

dominant position of industry in the Yugoslav economy, industrial cycles predetermine cycles in all other economic movements with the exception of agriculture.[5]

Similarly, much attention was devoted to organisational problems and difficulties. Enormous debate was generated around different economic reforms. These reforms were implemented only with difficulty. They produced what appeared to be a stop-go cycle of change. Whenever Yugoslavia attempted to integrate more closely with the world economy, the weak competitive position of Yugoslav industry produced pressure to protect it. The basic difficulty was put sharply by the Yugoslav economist Socan in 1967: 'On entering the world market intensively, more than one third of our industrial production would find the question of existence more acute than the question of growth.' There thus developed what one observer has called 'a series of cycles around the underlying trend towards centralisation, cycles of liberalisation, economic instability and further liberalisation'.[6]

None of this seemed to matter too much so long as each year saw strong growth, albeit at an uneven and slowly declining rate. The planners, the economists and the Western enthusiasts all argued as to the cause of the problems, but all seemed to assume that sooner or later a solution would be found, whether in the form of a new organisational framework, higher charges for capital to discipline investment, the break up of large firms or a more determined effort to integrate with the world market. The spirit of this era was well captured in 1971 by the Yugoslav economist Alexander Bajt when, having reviewed the evidence of cyclical instability, he concluded that it was primarily caused by policy and planning errors which would therefore disappear with increased knowledge and experience.[7] Nothing could have been further from the truth. As the world boom turned into stagnation in the 1970s so the great Yugoslav 'miracle' turned into the no less great Yugoslav 'nightmare'.

Yugoslavia had clearly benefited enormously from its closer integration in the 1950s and 60s with the booming world market. In Eastern Europe the stimulus to growth had been more indirect, in the form of competitive pressures on planners to push resources into high priority growth sectors. But in the Yugoslav case these planning pressures were supplemented by those of the world market (although still moderated by various protective devices). Once the boom disappeared, however, the Yugoslav economy felt the backlash of the world economy more sharply and directly than the other Eastern European economies. The source of its difficulties was only in part internal inefficiency. Although Yugoslavia had made considerable progress during the boom, it remained a relatively weak force in the world economy, as did all the economies at that level of development—Yugoslavia today has an output per head of some $2,000. The collapse of the boom left all these economies in highly vulnerable positions as the gale of competition increased.

The Yugoslav economy relied heavily on imports not only for fuel but for other essentials for its industry. Nearly two thirds of imports in the mid-1970s were raw materials and semi-manufactures. Some 55 percent of these came from the OECD countries and 16 percent from the developing world. Manufactured goods and manufactured exports therefore had a high import content. Overall more than half of Yugoslav exports were made up of agricultural goods and semi-manufactures and, reflecting the weaker export performance, only 42 percent of these went to the OECD countries, 16 percent to developing countries and 42 percent to the Eastern bloc.[8] Yugoslavia was also more closely tied to the world market through its export of labour. In 1966 all the restrictions on the outflow of labour power had been removed and Yugoslav workers had gone abroad in their hundreds of thousands. Emigrant remittances combined with tourist revenue were of major help in overcoming the virtually permanent balance of trade deficit. But when the migrants returned they naturally brought with them pressure to maintain their Western lifestyles, which fed back into more demand for Western imports, and because of the links with the West they had the cash to do this. In 1970, 18.4 percent of the financial assets of Yugoslav households were held in foreign currencies, and this figure had risen to 33.6 percent by 1975.[9] Integration also existed, albeit imperfectly, at the level of the capital market and through Yugoslav membership of the major international financial institutions. Yugoslavia, for example, had been a founding member of the International Monetary Fund.

Major signs of trouble began to emerge in the early 1970s, as they did in the rest of the world. The trade situation with the West turned sharply against Yugoslavia in 1974-76 with the oil price rise and related events. The Yugoslav export share sank and the terms of trade fell by 65 percent. The result was that export revenues crashed by as much as a quarter, costing, according to the OECD, some 3 to 4 percent of GDP. While this was happening the outflow of labour reached a peak in 1973-74 when the numbers of Yugoslavs working abroad were estimated at 25.5 percent of the domestic labour force. Then migration began to decline as conditions in Western Europe worsened, bringing home some of those who had migrated earlier. Unemployment, which had been only 4.2 percent in 1973, rose to a then record of 11 percent in 1976. Inflation, which at 1950s prices had been around 5 percent per year, rose to 12 percent in the 1960s and 17 percent in the 1970s.

The government responded to these first difficulties in a similar way to other governments. They tried to stimulate the domestic economy in the hope that growth would provide a way out of their difficulties. There was a huge investment push, and by 1978 gross capital formation reached 40 percent of gross social product. But the earlier external conditions of growth were no longer there. Imports were sucked in as exports became more difficult to sell. It was estimated that every 1 percent fall in the growth of the advanced West reduced Yugoslav exports by 1 to 1.6 percent.[10] Like an insect caught in a spider's web, the Yugoslav ruling class twisted and turned but only seemed to get more entangled in the world crisis. The balance of payments deficit shot up to 6 percent of GNP in 1979 and international borrowing was resorted to on a major scale. The result was that when the world economy went down again in the early 1980s it brought the Yugoslav economy to its knees.

A vicious circle of crisis, stagnation, unemployment, inflation, devaluation and debt has lasted throughout the 1980s. In particular the growing crisis has driven Yugoslavia into the arms of the International Monetary Fund and the Western banks, which have acted to powerfully reinforce the internal demands for more market discipline. By 1982 Yugoslavia was paying 8 percent of its GNP and 23 percent of its export earnings in debt service. And with Poland and Romania it experienced even greater debt difficulties. The situation was reached where, in the words of a Yugoslav commentator, 'For all practical purposes, Yugoslavia's reduced foreign liquidity at the end of 1982 resulted in the international capital market's refusal to advance further loans to Yugoslav borrowers'.[11]

The IMF was the only alternative. In 1979 IMF debt had been only 2 per cent of Yugoslavia's total debt, but by 1983 it had risen to 11 percent. Yugoslavia was able to take advantage of a succession of standby credits. The most important, for $2.2 billion, came in 1981. Subsequently, as the government implemented an austerity programme to cope with the crisis, it was able to negotiate terms with

Western commercial banks and governments. All of these deals put more pressure on the economy and the working class. Typical were the terms that came from the IMF in 1981:

> The conditions under which Yugoslavia was advanced a loan included the curtailment of domestic demand, channelling investments towards priority sectors to improve the production structure and boost exports, reduction of the balance of payment on current account deficit, realistic dinar exchange rate, and introduction of austerity policies in the monetary credit field.[12]

Yet these measures have not been able to turn the economy around. At best they have been a holding operation. The pressure on Yugoslav society has been relentless. What the newspaper *Borba* called 'hard times' in 1982 have come to characterise the decade as a whole, as can be seen in tables 1 and 2.

Table 1
Yugoslavia—signs of crisis: the external account[13]

	Balance of trade (US$ millions)	Balance of payments (US$ millions)	Total debt (US$ millions)
1979	-105	-3,665	14,952
1980	-85	-2,316	18,395
1981	-60	-961	20,168
1982	-18	-475	20,260
1983	-9	+275	20,501
1984	-3.5	+504	20,191
1985	-2	+800	19,891
1986	-2	+1,000	-

Yet in the late 1980s there is still no sight of a solution to these problems. The proposals of the Krajger Commission for a long run stabilisation resulted in a superhuman effort to get a grip on the economy in 1983-85. But, as the tables show, in 1986 the whole situation began to get out of hand again. Things have simply got worse since then.[15] From the point of view of those in control, the country had, in the words of the United Nations Economic Commission on Europe, 'entered a phase in which there was no effective mechanism to bring about macro-economic structural adjustment'.[16]

The external pressures on the economy have been maintained as attempts to control the balance of trade deficit have failed. Debt is now $20 billion with no sign of its underlying cause being dealt with. Whereas between 1971 and 1978 the exports of goods and services grew at 17.9 percent while interest payments grew at 16.5 percent, since then (in the period 1979-86) the export of goods and services has grown at only 6 percent compared to a growth of interest payments at a rate of 13 percent.[17] And there is no sign of a turnaround in the domestic economy. Labour productivity is still only at the level of the mid-1970s, while the investment rate is down to around 20 percent. At the same time the economy is on the brink of hyperinflation. Inflation was brought down to 10-15 percent in 1984-85 but rose to 115 percent in 1986, 130 percent in 1987 and is predicted for 200 percent in 1988. In reaction to this Yugoslavs have moved even more of their savings into foreign currencies, holding only around two fifths of household financial assets in dinars.

But the real cost of all of this is to be measured in the years of austerity suffered by the working class. Table 2 shows how personal consumption has fared. In 1980-81 real incomes crashed by 13 percent, and since then consumption and incomes have continued to be held down. Unemployment has also worsened dramatically. Already in the

Table 2
Yugoslavia—signs of crisis: the internal record[14]

	Index per head in 1972 prices (1979 = 100) of			Unemployment %	Retail price index (1979 = 100)
	national income	investment	personal consumption		
1970	64	59	67	-	23
1979	100	100	100	11.9	100
1980	101	93	100	11.9	131
1981	101	84	97	11.9	189
1982	101	78	96	12.4	248
1983	99	70	94	12.8	843
1984	100	63	92	13.3	554
1985	99	60	92	13.8	944
1986	102	61	95	14.3	1,775

early 1970s the self management theorist Vanek called unemployment one of 'the darkest aspects of the economy'.[18] At that time the rate was only some 5 to 6 percent and there were over a million Yugoslav workers abroad. As the crisis has intensified so the unemployment figures have climbed and the numbers abroad declined.

None of this is likely to change. The rulers of Yugoslavia have rejected what is called 'a state of siege'—'the zero option' of closing the door to the outside world—an option which offers nothing to ordinary Yugoslavs. But the pressure is therefore to move to a more radical structuring which also can only be achieved by intensifying the pressure on workers. The most adventurous Yugoslav rationalisers are calling for a 'bonfire of controls'. They argue that the problem with the rise in unemployment is that it has not been sharp enough to effect the necessary restructuring—whole sections of industry need to be allowed to collapse. But how much unemployment would suffice? No one knows. The Yugoslav economist Mencinger estimated that throughout the 1970s nearly 20 percent of those in jobs were effectively redundant in terms of their real contribution to the economy.[19] Allowing for those already without jobs, many of whom are young long term unemployed, what is clearly being suggested is unemployment of 30 percent or more, to be combined with more cuts in the real standard of living.

Not surprisingly, Yugoslav workers have not been quiescent in the face of this. Strikes, of which there were less than 100 in 1983, rose to 699 in 1985 and 851 in 1986. Then in March 1987 a wage freeze followed by price rises brought strikes and demonstrations. Further price rises in November 1987 saw protest on an even more significant scale. Over 1987 as a whole there were 1,570 strikes involving some 365,000 workers— equivalent to one in ten of the whole workforce. The pressure continued into 1988 with strikes in the first half of the year running at twice the level for the same period in 1987.[20] The market would seem therefore to have brought Yugoslavia to the brink—but to the brink of what? For what have also been created are powerful counter-currents which are seeking to divert protest into a frenzy of nationalism.

Towards the disintegration of Yugoslavia?

So far our discussion has neglected the enormous regional differences in Yugoslavia, but, as anyone who followed events in that country in 1988 will know, these are central to the nature of the Yugoslav crisis. Regional differences in Yugoslavia are certainly as great, and probably greater, than those in any other advanced country. Yugoslavia is divided into six republics and two autonomous provinces. The greatest contrast is between the most advanced republic of Slovenia and the most backward province of Kosovo. Yugoslav economists liken the existence of these two extremes to having both West Germany and India in the same country, and this is confirmed by even the most casual glance at the regional data. Slovenia, for example, has a per capita income six times greater than that of Kosovo, and is to all intents and purposes a region almost as advanced as much of Western Europe. The birth rate is low at 13.8 per 1,000, Slovenians live in small families—the average size of household in 3.18. Illiteracy has virtually been eliminated, with only 0.8 percent illiterate compared to the Yugoslav average of 9.5 percent. The facilities and standard of living have reached a level expected in an advanced area. There is one doctor for every 407 inhabitants, nursery places for 36.2 percent of the children and the infant death rate is 13.3 per 1,000. Some 92.5 percent of homes have a water supply and sewerage, 73.8 percent have bathrooms and 42.3 percent central heating. Now compare this with Kosovo. Here the birth rate of 30 per 1,000 is the highest in Europe. Household size is 6.92. The infant death rate is 55.8 per 1,000. There is one doctor for every 1,013 people and nursery places for only 2.5 percent of the children. Illiteracy runs at nearly twice the national average at 17.6 percent. Only 43.3 percent of homes have a water supply and sewerage, 27.1 percent bathrooms and a mere 5.8 percent central heating.[21]

Major inequalities were inherited by the new regime after the Second World War, and these have proved impervious to efforts to change them. Efforts have been made. In the years 1949-85, for example, 54 percent of loans coming from the International Bank for Reconstruction and Development went into the underdeveloped areas of the country.[22] They have been negated, however, by the strength of market forces and the fact that the state, in order to compete in the world economy, has had to tailor its programmes to the needs of Yugoslav capital as a whole rather then the needs of particular parts of the population. This is the root of the inability of the state to overcome the unevenness in the economy, as can be seen in table 3 overleaf.

What the market has done on top of this has been to encourage a degree of economic disintegration of Yugoslavia into its constituent republics. If we take the 1970s as an example, inter-regional trade fell from 27.4 percent of all trade in 1970 to 22.2 percent in 1980. Thus the various republics do the majority of their trade internally and

Table 3			
Index of regional social product per capita[23]			
	1947	*1965*	*1985*
Yugoslavia	100	100	100
Slovenia	163	183	203
Croatia	108	120	125
Vojvodina	117	112	118
*Serbia proper**	97	96	99
Montenegro	71	76	78
Bosnia-Hercegovina	80	72	69
Macedonia	69	67	64
Kosovo	50	36.5	28
*excluding the autonomous provinces of Kosovo and Vojvodina			

externally, but not with one another. The percentage of exports going from the regions to other Yugoslav regions fell from 40 percent to 31 percent in the same period. Similarly, enterprises are almost entirely based within republics, minimising links between them. This has meant a high degree of economic fragmentation in Yugoslav society. Different regional sections of the ruling class have been quick to use these divisions to their own advantage. In Slovenia, the most advanced republic, for example, the ideology of the market is especially strong—in part because it is sponsored by a leadership that is confident that a highly developed area situated in a triangle formed by Austria, Hungary and Italy could survive a 'bonfire of controls'. Its leadership therefore constantly attacks the rest of Yugoslavia for its profligacy, for building expensive 'white elephant' industrial plants, and for encouraging corruption. That this has taken place on a massive scale is undoubted, but the solution is not the market—as can be seen from the estimate that a bonfire of controls would cut the standard of living in Kosovo by as much as 35-45 percent.[24] This sort of pressure has, however, fed tendencies towards political disintegration. At one level it has produced a significant political differentiation across Yugoslavia—Slovenia, for example, is renowned for its political liberalism and for offering a haven to those persecuted in the rest of the country. But much more negatively it has also enormously encouraged the traditional tendencies of nationalism whose objective base the regime never succeeded in removing.

Yugoslavia was formed out of the expansion of Serbia which, once it had become freed from the Ottoman Empire, quickly incorporated its surrounding territory. During the inter-war years Yugoslavia (which had been formed in 1918-19) was ruled by King Alexander, who preached 'Yugoslavism' but frequently practised a 'Greater Serbia' policy which particularly worked against the Croat population. This led to bloody internecine warfare during the Second World War. After the war Tito's regime claimed that the League of Communists had become the new 'connective tissue' of a genuinely Yugoslav 'nation'. But, unable to deal with the fundamental inequalities, Tito's own nightmare was said to be that the League would turn into six separate Communist parties. The weak identification with 'Yugoslavia' today is shown by the 1981 census, where out of 22.3 million people only 1.2 million declared themselves to be 'Yugoslav'. While this was many more than the 1971 figure of 273,000, it meant that the vast majority of Yugoslavs still identified more with their regions (those declaring that they knew no country were fewest of all).[25] Significantly amongst Slovenians, Macedonians and Albanians (in Kosovo) Yugoslav identification was even weaker.

Nationalism has historically been used by the party bosses to obtain more power. It has been countered by a Yugoslav nationalism aiming to hold the country together. The latter, however, has often been seen simply as Serbism, given that Serbia is the historical core of the country and the Serbs the biggest group. A major crisis erupted in 1971 with mass nationalist Croat protests. Demonstrations were held with slogans like 'Stop the plunder of Croatia' and 'End the retention quotas' (this latter referring to the then practice of requiring firms to deposit 90 percent of their foreign exchange earnings with the national bank). The ideology of 'self management' was also used as a cloak for nationalism, with various leaders arguing that it meant that workers (ie their enterprises) should retain all of their profits rather than have a proportion of them redistributed. This crisis was overcome by constitutional reform, which increased Yugoslavian federalism. So long as Tito was alive the different tendencies were held in check, but after his death, with the impact of the growing crisis, the problem has exploded again. This time the problem is the relation of Serbia to its autonomous province of Kosovo.

Although there has been a majority of Albanians in Kosovo since Yugoslavia was formed in 1918, Kosovo is still claimed as the traditional heartland of ancient Serbia. It was at the Battle of Kosovo in 1389 that Serbia was defeated by the Turks and integrated into the Ottoman

Empire for the next five centuries. But much has changed since then, and today 77.5 percent of the population of Kosovo is Albanian and Muslim while only 18.3 percent is Serbian. As we have seen, Kosovo is one of the poorest areas in the whole of Europe, but that has not stopped the Serbian leaders whipping up anti-Albanian feeling on the grounds that it is Serbs who are being exploited and oppressed. During 1988, led by the Serbian party leader Slobodan Milosevic, there have at times been almost daily mass demonstrations for the reintegration of Kosovo into Serbia. These have overflowed with racist hostility to the Albanian population of Kosovo. Slogans like 'Give us arms', 'We'll kill anyone who disagrees with Slobodan', and stories and rumours of attacks, rapes and child molestation by Albanians appear to have created an almost pogrom like atmosphere. This strikes not only at Kosovo, but also threatens the other Yugoslav republics with the spectre of a 'Greater Serbia' asserting its power over them as well.

This stimulation of nationalist fervour arises directly from the crisis and is in part an attempt to divert working class protest. But at the same time the strengthening of that protest is the best protection against such nationalism developing further. This, of course, exposes the con-tradictory position of an opposition to the regime which has been se-duced by the appeal of the market. The result is a potentially dangerous paralysis. There is the added possibility that, instead of standing out against the reactionary aspects of nationalism, the opposition might look to saviours from outside. Thus one source 'close to the dissidents' has been quoted as saying:

> The army is the last bastion of a united Yugoslavia now in the process
> of disintegration and we must keep it intact by all means and whatever
> the cost.[26]

It is not at all clear how typical this idea is; hopefully it is quite un-representative. But what is clear is that the army is standing in the wings (incidentally with a predominance of Serbian NCOs). The threat of a coup has already been raised. In Slovenia in 1988 the mag-azine *Mladina* revealed secret plans, including arrest lists, to bring the republic into line. Whether this was a serious coup attempt that was forestalled or sections of the army trying to frighten the Slovenian leadership away from its liberal position is not clear. But we should simply note that the people who were arrested as a result of this were those who revealed the plans, and not those who made them.

At the time of writing it is not clear how the Yugoslav nightmare will develop. The crisis may be temporarily overcome, it may develop as a consequence of even more rampant nationalism, or workers' protests may increase and cut the ground away from reaction. But for this to happen it is all the more necessary that socialists expose the myth of the market.

The illusion of self management

The 'market socialist' argument is not only mistaken about the economic possibilities of the market, but also about the possibility of it conferring real power on the working class. Part of the attraction of 'market socialism' has been the belief that it could be linked to workers' democracy. Workers could control their enterprises but these would then relate to one another through the market. This argument exists in a positive and a negative form, and we will treat each separately. The positive form is that self management can be advanced by removing private property and allowing workers to elect their own managers, if possible from amongst themselves. A society of self managed firms could then develop linked by the invisible hand of the market.

Throughout history there have been many such schemes, going back to the utopian socialists with their ideals of 'a republic of the workshop'. But all these schemes have been intended to be implemented from above under the protection of intellectuals, wealthy benefactors or benevolent states. This is indicative of the real lack of workers' power that they involve. Even if it were true that self management and the market gave power to the workers (and, as we shall see, it is not true), it would still be the case that 'that which has been given can just as easily be taken back'.

The classic example of the attempted imposition of self management from above and the consequent lack of real workers' power can be found in Yugoslavia. Here there is no dispute as to the origin of the whole idea of self management. It was simply the idea of four people. The story has been told a number of times by Milovan Djilas. According to Djilas, in 1949, when he was at the very top of the Yugoslav leadership, he worked out the basic idea in a half hour discussion with Eduard Kardelj and Boris Kidric. The idea was put to Tito who after some initial hesitation suddenly seemed to grasp the idea and declared, 'Ah, I see what it is—factories to the workers.' A few months later he put the Workers Self Management Bill to the National Assembly, where of course it was passed automatically on 26 June 1950.[27] There was no pretence that self management was a product of working class struggle. Indeed, the dissident philosopher Svetozar Stojanovic once reported the existence of a factory plaque which declared, 'The party-state leadership *gave* the factories to the management of workers' collectives'.[28] Subsequently self management developed through various stages, the latest of which came in the mid-1970s with the creation of self management units called BOALs or Basic Organisations of Associated Labour. These can operate either at the level of the whole enterprise or divisions of it.

Today the idea that Yugoslav workers have any real power is hardly taken seriously at all. Workers' rights look impressive on paper, but the evidence that the real situation is not any different from elsewhere is overwhelming. This is so whether we look at objective indicators (including the evidence of crisis we have already discussed) or subjective ones. That effective managerial control exists has long been established. The evidence is glaring: at a Congress of Self Managers only 80 out of the 1,200 delegates were manual workers![29] Even official sources admit that membership of the League of Communists is a vehicle for careerists. Thus one official source, explaining the increase in Communist Party membership in the 1970s from one in 14 adults to one in seven notes:

> League of Communist membership was identified with moral and po-
> litical fitness, so that a number of young and other people joined the
> League to obtain a job or be promoted to responsible and managerial
> posts more easily.[30]

Equally, studies of income distribution have shown the inequality inbuilt in Yugoslav society is as great as in other countries. This must directly undercut the argument that the working class has any greater power in Yugoslavia.

But perhaps one of the most obvious signs of the lack of real power of the working class is to be found in the much discussed subject of corruption. This is sometimes treated as an unfortunate blemish on Yugoslav society, but it is more serious than this. What it really reflects is the absence of any real control from below—otherwise corruption could not develop on the scale that it has. This corruption takes many forms. While Tito was alive it was particularly obvious in what Djilas called his 'appetite for the fashionably acceptable…his royal way of life'. It was reflected, too, in the personality cult that grew up around him which, if it did not reach heights known in other Eastern European countries, still had more than its share of ridiculous adulation. But the corruption runs more deeply than this. In 1987 its scale came to light in the notorious Agro-Commerce Affair. Agro-Commerce was a large agri-business which had been issuing dud cheques and promissory notes to improve its position and line the pockets of its management. And it was not only the management who were implicated, but also their protectors, including the local party bosses and the Yugoslav vice-president. Some $200 million worth of cheques and notes were outstanding, threatening the whole economy. Investigations made estimates of similar rackets by other managements worth anywhere between $900 and $2,000 million. Not surprisingly workers' views, and their behaviour, reflect their fundamental alienation from the system. As one worker said of his rights under self management, 'That is on paper. When the managers choose their people, the workers have to obey. That's how it is here'.[31]

But why is 'socialist market self management' such a fraud? For its supporters the answer would be that the basic idea is sound—the problem is the unpropitious Yugoslav circumstances. Thus Djilas has argued, 'In the context of a monolithic party, an omnipotent secret police, and an autocratic leader, self management could not effectively become democratic'.[32] But the problem goes far deeper than this. The very essence of the market is to deny workers the power that 'self management' seeks to give them.

This is so in three senses. Firstly, although the theorists of 'self management' stress giving workers choice, the reality of the market is to remove that choice. Production for profit requires that the internal organisation of the firm be subordinated to the external object of profit maximisation (even if this is constrained in various ways). Indeed, in the pure market model no one has any choice at all. In their work they are simply factors of production shunted around to achieve the optimum profit. The fact that the real world is not like this does not alter the fact that the market still appears as a coercive external force:

> In accordance with market rationality, self management has received a new content, which at the same time tends to render self management unnecessary. Workers can have their share in management, but profit production does not really need the voices of the workers in decision making. This is the bitter irony of the market self management model… Workers, instead of being only small cog wheels, become bigger ones in

a market self management machine which is neither run by them nor run in their interests.[33]

Moreover, this judgement extends not just to the power of workers within their 'own' firms but to society as a whole. This was pointed out by Stojanovic in his early critique of Yugoslav society. But even he was unwilling to draw the conclusion that Yugoslavia was a capitalist society:

> So long as it exists, the market will try to impose itself over society as the supreme regulator and criterion of human relations... It thus comes into conflict with the mission of the socialist community, which seeks to humanise existing need and develop new, human needs... Without rational control of economic tendencies by the associated producers, socialism in Marx's sense is out of the question.[34]

And if 'socialist market self management' denies workers' power, it also does nothing about the underlying exploitation and alienation of capitalism. These are not removed by simply appointing worker managers who are rooted in capitalism as a mode of production. As Herbert Marcuse, describing the power that bourgeois democracy gave to workers, once put it, to allow slaves to elect their masters does not alter their status as slaves.[35] Similarly, to allow workers in a system dominated by capitalist competition to elect their managers and have a share of profits does not alter their fundamental status as wage slaves. Nor does it change the nature of that society or make it socialist.

But once the concepts of socialism and capitalism are emptied of their content in this way it becomes possible to pass self management off as 'humanisation', possible to set off on a bizarre journey in which the maximisation of human freedom becomes identified with the maximum subordination to the market—an idea dear to the heart of every right wing economist in the West. Thus Boris Kidric argued that nationalisation and self management meant that commodity production in Yugoslavia had become 'socialist commodity production'. It was then only a short step for another theorist of the socialist market, Milentije Popovic, to argue that 'the freer are commodities in the process of production, the more independent the economic laws of society, to that extent man is...also freer and more independent'.[36]

This is bad enough, but the illusion of self management goes one step further. Not only does it deny workers real power, but it also atomises their class interests by forcing them to look to their own enterprise, seeing their fellow workers in other firms as competitors.

Thus in Yugoslavia, Stojanovic noted, 'Mired in the framework of self governing groups, the working class cannot make its way on to the political stage to pose questions concerning the total distribution of surplus value.' To this we would want to add only that it is not just the distribution but the production of surplus that is of vital importance. Stojanovic then went on to add, 'So long as this is the case, the burden of economic reform will fall most heavily on the shoulders of the working class'.[37]

But the argument about the market also comes in a negative form, especially from those in opposition in Eastern Europe and those forced into emigration:

> Any consistently non-market economy must be, by definition: centralised; run by the command plan; controlled by a handful of planners rather than the workers themselves; based on manipulation of the producers by the planning board.[38]

> To demand self management without economic restraints is to relapse into utopianism and *birokratizm*. Democratic norms are obtainable only by real forms of decision making and not on the basis of utopianism towards real needs. It cannot be built without a market and market competition.[39]

Such arguments could be multiplied without end. They spring from societies where the state has dominated, controlled and squeezed political life out of existence for so long. But for all this they still rest on error. Markets do not bring political freedom, nor do they guarantee it. Historically the coincidence of markets and freedom has always been rare. Even today Amnesty International estimates that 90 out of 135 countries it investigates violate human rights in one way or another. While this includes all of the state capitalist economies, it also includes the vast majority of capitalist market economies too. Political freedom in those countries where bourgeois democracy has been won is a product of protest and struggle. It is maintained by the strength of the labour movement. This is why when that labour movement is pushed back, when, as in Britain for example, the ideology of the market is used to undercut and divert attention away from the struggle for socialism, then the strong state rises up on the back of defeat.

Notes

1   Relations with Russia during the war are best summed up in a famous telegram sent by Tito to Moscow: 'If you cannot understand what a hard time we are having, and if you cannot help us, at least do not hinder us.' Quoted in P Auty, *Tito: a Biography* (1970), p214.

2   According to Roy Medvedev, the following note from Tito was found in Stalin's desk after he died: 'Comrade Stalin, I request that you stop sending terrorists to Yugoslavia to kill me. We have already caught seven men, one with a revolver, another with a grenade, the third with a bomb… If this does not stop, I will send one to Moscow and there will be no need to send another.' R Medvedev, *On Stalin and Stalinism* (1979), p145.

3   For a useful up to date discussion of Yugoslav development by someone who shared some of this initial enthusiasm see B MacFarlane, *Yugoslavia, Economics, Politics, Society* (1988).

4   See, for example, A Sapir, 'Economic Growth and Factor Substitution: What Happened to the Yugoslav Miracle', *Economic Journal*, vol 90 (June 1980), and the reply by the eminent Yugoslav economist Alexander Bajt, 'Economic Growth and Factor Substitution…: Some Comments', *Economic Journal*, vol 96 (December 1986).

5   B Horvat, *Business Cycles in Yugoslavia* (1971), pp228-229.

6   Quoted in D Flaherty, 'Economic Reform and Foreign Trade in Yugoslavia', *Cambridge Journal of Economics*, vol 6 (1982), p120-122.

7   A Bajt, 'Investment Cycles in European Socialist Economies: a Review Article', *Journal of Economic Literature*, vol 9 (1971), pp53-64.

8   D Flaherty, op cit.

9   Ibid; M Bleaney, *Do Socialist Economies Work?* (1988), p151.

10 L D'Andrea Tyson, *The Yugoslav Economic System and its Performance in the 1970s* (1980), p92. 'Gross capital formation' involves all investment in new and replacement machinery and buildings. 'Gross social product' was widely used in the former Yugoslavia as a measure of total output. It is analagous to Western output concepts but includes some double counting.

11 'Cooperation With International Financial Organisations 1944-1985', *Yugoslav Survey*, vol 27, no 4 (1986), p70.

12 Ibid, p69.

13 *Statistichi Godisnjak Jugoslavie 1987* [*Statistical Pocket Book of Yugoslavia 1987*].

14 Ibid.

15 B MacFarlane, op cit, p138.

16 Quoted in M Bleaney, op cit, p139.

17 'Yugoslavia's Balance of Payments and External Debt, 1971-1986', *Yugoslav Survey*, vol 27, no 4 (1987), p66.

18 J Vanek, *The Labour Managed Economy* (1977).

19 Quoted in A Bajt, 'Factor Substitution', op cit, p1,087.

20 'The Belgrade Road', *Socialist Review* 111, July-August 1986.

21 *Statistical Pocket Book of Yugoslavia 1987*, op cit.

22 'Cooperation With International Financial Organisations', op cit, p73.

23 Data for 1947 from D Milenkovitch, *Plan and Market in Yugoslav Economic Thought* (1971), p181; for 1965 and 1985 from *Statistical Pocket Book of Yugoslavia 1987*, op cit, p53.

24 *Guardian*, 26 September 1988.

25 *Statistical Pocket Book of Yugoslavia 1987*, op cit, p37.

26 Quoted in the *Guardian*, 13 June 1988.

27 M Djilas, *The Unperfect Society* (1971), p158. See also his *Tito* (1980), p45.

28 Quoted in G Sher, *Praxis: Marxist Criticism and Dissent in Socialist Yugoslavia* (1977), p155. Stojanovic was a leading member of the 'Praxis Group'—a number of academics based around a journal sharply critical of both Stalinism and Yugoslav society. They were, however, rather more ready to condemn the former wholesale than the latter.

29 B MacFarlane, op cit, p225.

30 'Membership of the League of Communists of Yugoslavia', *Yugoslav Survey*, vol 23, no 4 (1982), p27.

31 M Djilas, *Tito*, op cit, p21 and ch 9. Djilas notes that the Belgrade branch of the Socialist Alliance proposed Tito for the 4th Order of the National Hero for endurance after a successful operation! On the Agro-Commerce affair and for the workers' response see B MacFarlane, op cit, pp159, 171.

32 M Djilas, op cit, p74.

33 P Bihari 'Hungary: Towards a Socialist Market Economy?', *Studies in Economy*, no 18 (Autumn 1985), pp31-33.

34 S Stojanovic, *Between Ideals and Reality: A Critique of Socialism and its Future* (1973), p170.

35 We are not suggesting, of course, that there was no difference between bourgeois democracy and slavery.

36 Quoted in D Milenkovitch, op cit, p95.

37 S Stojanovic, op cit, p119.

38 R Selucky, 'Marxism and Self Management', in J Vanek (ed), *Self Management Economic Liberation of Man* (1975), p58. Selucky was forced into exile from Eastern Europe.

39 Radisav Marinkovic, a Yugoslav reformer, quoted in B MacFarlane, op cit, p74. An essentially similar position is taken by the Hungarians A Helier and F Feher in *Dictatorship over Needs* (1983) and *Eastern Left, Western Left: Totalitarianism, Freedom and Democracy* (1987).

Chapter 2

Cauldron of discontent

Duncan Blackie

Yugoslavia is a frontline state in the world crisis, as its leaders admitted to the world at last month's central committee meeting.

The statistics speak for themselves: over 200 percent inflation and *official* unemployment running at 15 percent. In some areas it is as high as 50 percent, with another quarter of the workforce having to seek employment in Western Europe. The foreign debt stands at over $1,000 for every Yugoslav. Average earnings are just $120 a month. Real living standards have fallen by 15 percent over the last year, and output this August was 1.3 percent down.

Lest there be any doubt about the scale of the crisis now hitting the country, the central committee of the League of Communists of Yugoslavia made it quite plain at their meeting last month. The country was on the edge of an abyss as the result of 'ignorance, corruption and bureaucracy', said Communist Party leader Stipe Suvar. Others, such as presidium (cabinet) member Vasil Tupurkovski, insisted that Yugoslavia was now at the low point of a two decade long slide into economic chaos and stagnation.

The meeting decided on three reforms.

The first is an intensification of 'market socialism', which roughly means an unfettered working of the market justified by a ruling bureaucracy in the stolen language of Marxism. Uneconomic enterprises must go to the wall—as must the poor, the old and the sick, as state spending is to be slashed. The period of large state subsidised industrial enterprises built in the poor south will be a thing of the past. Now, backward regions like Macedonia, Kosovo and Montenegro must open themselves up to the icy blast of world economic competition.

First published November 1988

Never mind that the debt, unemployment, declining living standards and raging inflation are all products of 'market socialism'—Yugoslavia's leaders are going to push the country through a massive shakeout, leading to even more misery.

In the republic of Croatia local party bosses estimate that the savings from the 'unburdening of the economy' will be equal to the entire profit made in the republic.

There have already been 800 strikes in the first half of this year. So Yugoslavia's rulers hope to get away with these new attacks by purging whole sections of the establishment and holding them responsible for the ills, and by continuing to focus discontent into a campaign against certain national minorities.

There is to be a review of the status of the component parts of Serbia. At present, under the 1974 constitution, there are two autonomous provinces within the borders of Serbia—Vojvodina, with a large proportion of ethnic Romanians and Hungarians living alongside Serbs, and Kosovo, with its overwhelming majority of ethnic Albanians.

And, to give a slightly more democratic gloss to the whole process, Suvar has said he wants a review of the relationship between party and state. He holds out the promise not of a multi-party state, but a 'no party state'.

Serbian party boss Slobodan Milosevic had hoped that the leadership of Kosovo would be removed and his plans for a Greater Serbia steamrollered through. But a coalition of the leaders of other republics saw to it that there was a slightly different outcome.

Four members of the politburo resigned, but only one was bumped, a Serb and key supporter of Milosevic, Dusan Ckerbic. Fifty members—over a third—of the central committee were purged as part of a process of 'cadre renewal'.

Other leaders are certainly worried by the populist campaign led by Milosevic. Croatian leader Vlado Ravlic has accused him of using 'Goebbels' methods', and of a 'Phalangist approach'.

But Milosevic has still succeeded in shifting the balance of the argument in his direction. Virtually every speaker denounced the elusive 'counter-revolution' in Kosovo, a racist slur on Albanians.

Suvar told the central committee, 'A counter-revolutionary coup is written on the flag of Albanian nationalism in Kosovo and everywhere in Yugoslavia where there have been greater concentrations of the Albanian nationality since the Second World War.'

And in backing the economic reforms which were especially wanted by the leaders of the prosperous republics of Croatia and Slovenia, he received their tacit backing in return for more attacks on other nationalities, just so long as it was not them.

Even the Kosovan leaders have made efforts to accommodate Milosevic. A total of 5,000 people have been thrown out of the local party in recent months for 'separatist deviations'.

But these moves can give Yugoslavia's rulers no more than a breathing space. They are sitting on top of a cauldron of discontent, which manifests itself in a mixture of nationalism and plain class hatred. Up to now the mixture has been manageable, but the proportions are ever shifting, and the measures needed to improve the economy and meet tight IMF guidelines are sure to continue to throw up revolts.

So serious is the crisis that many commentators are talking of the prospect of the country falling apart. According to the *Guardian*, a political disaster in Yugoslavia 'might put Mr Gorbachev off his reformist stroke and inspire widespread desperation throughout Eastern Europe'.

A destabilised Yugoslavia would indeed have massive repercussions way beyond its borders. According to the agreement between Stalin and Churchill in 1945 Yugoslavia was to be split '50/50' between East and West. In fact it asserted its independence with the Stalin-Tito split in 1948.

Since then, both sides have rested quite happy that the most important of the Balkan states is stable, if in neither camp. Neither of the superpowers can now be happy at the possibility of the destabilisation of one of the key pivots in the central European divide.

However, countries do not just 'fall apart'. An existing state embodies massive vested economic, political and personal interests. When the majority of central committee members spoke last month of the need to hold Yugoslavia together it was more than just a good line in rhetoric.

Milosevic may have little liking for the Slovenian or Croatian leaders, but he will not want to see the ending of the massive foreign receipts that come in from these areas. With only 8 percent of the population, Slovenia accounts for 20 percent of GNP, and an even greater proportion of desperately needed foreign currency receipts.

Slovenian leader Milan Kucan may want economic independence for his relatively prosperous republic to create a second Switzerland or Austria, but he will not want Slovenia to just abandon the benefits of being part of a larger state.

For the Serbian leaders the only 'falling apart' which would make political sense is one in which they won effective colonial control over the smaller southern republics as well.

None of these changes are likely to take place without the most massive ructions. As a general rule, states do not divide short of an all out civil war, and there is little reason to suspect that Yugoslavia's republics will come to an amicable separation.

Just how bloody the situation could get was shown in 1981 when tanks rumbled through the streets of the Kosovan capital, Pristina, and killed 300 to put down an Albanian revolt.

For now, however, Belgrade is not Beirut. Workers are fighting their bosses as well as being encouraged to fight each other. Which tendency will come to dominate is not yet decided.

Chapter 3

The wrong enemy

Duncan Blackie

Slobodan Milosevic, the leader of the Serbian Communist Party and the reactionary Serbian nationalist movement, spoke before an estimated one million people in Belgrade last month. He called for the autonomous provinces of Kosovo and Vojvodina to be subsumed into Serbia, the largest of the Yugoslavian republics.

His campaign is characterised by plain racism. 'Death to Albanians' is one of the commonest cries on the pro-Milosevic demonstrations. He says there has been an exodus of Serbs from Kosovo, due to the 'systematic campaign of terror and genocide' being waged by Albanian separatists. But the first Albanian demonstrations in Kosovo did not take place until the start of Milosevic's second round of Serbian rallies, and after two of the Kosovan Communist Party leaders had been forcibly removed by his pressure. Milosevic told the recent Belgrade rally that he would be prepared to sanction military action against Kosovo if necessary.

Milosevic claims, 'Children are raped, houses set on fire, tombs desecrated and an entire culture blotted out.' But the real oppression in Yugoslavia is *against* the Albanians, not by them. State radio now reports migrant building workers being hounded out of Belgrade and at least one Serbian local authority banning the sale of houses between nationalities, which bars Albanians from moving in.

The reason Milosevic is so powerful is that he *appears* to offer a real solution to the woes of ordinary workers. He speaks of the need to improve the economy by removing resistance to reform from comfortably off bureaucrats. This is then mixed in with racism.

This combination was used when mass rallies succeeded in removing the government of Vojvodina in October. Workers turned up outside the parliament building demanding both an end to their crushing economic misery and a Greater Serbia.

First published December 1988

The demonstrators were given a boost by Milosevic when he refused pleas by the Vojvodina government to deploy police against the demonstrators. The party leaders had ordered a cooling off period. A planned million strong rally in Belgrade was called off in October. All the party leaders, including Milosevic, had decided that bringing workers out onto the stage of politics was an extremely dangerous business. Once out they would not easily be persuaded to return.

No party leader wants Yugoslav workers to get into the habit of invading the national parliament building (which they have done three times in as many weeks). An indication of the danger of these developments was shown when Milosevic's supporters tried to get rid of the Montenegrin government. The demonstrators were attacked by riot police.

Two days later, according to state controlled radio:

> Working class Niksic is seething with political and social tensions. Numerous sessions of various bodies, official and unofficial meetings and gatherings of workers and students are being held in the town. In this unusual atmosphere few people are carrying out their ordinary everyday tasks.

As the Communist Party leader in the northern republic of Slovenia, Milan Kucan, said:

> It is not hard to stoke the fire of political, national, social and other passions, but we should remember how slowly oblivion puts them out. It is high time to sober up, to stop the mindlessness that is pushing us into catastrophe.

Another measure of the crisis is continual speculation about a coup in one or more parts of the country. There was almost certainly one planned for last spring in Slovenia.

This would be a costly option and it is not certain who would carry out the coup, or who it would back. Some 70 percent of the officer corps is Serbian. But the top officers also owe their power and prestige to being highly placed within the Yugoslav state, not a republic a third of its size.

There should be no doubt that Yugoslav workers are suffering, and prepared to fight back. But *how* they revolt depends on their political ideas. Tragically, the only significant political force organising among the working class is the bureaucracy itself. There could be no clearer argument for the need for independent socialist politics in the working class.

Chapter 4

Back to the Balkans

Duncan Blackie

Ethnic conflict in Yugoslavia has entered a new phase with the upsurge of struggle between Serbs and Croats in the republic of Croatia. The complex mix of communal tensions makes Yugoslavia a special case in Eastern Europe, but also a grim reminder of what could lie in store for other countries in the region if they are consigned to economic stagnation.

Struggle flared in Croatia in August and September, when local Serbs sealed off the region around the town of Knin. They closed roads and railways to the region and took large quantities of arms from the police station, including 100 automatic and semi-automatic rifles. They also organised demonstrations against the possible reorganisation of the police units in Knin, who quite willingly handed over their weapons to the rioters, as 97 percent of them are Serbs.

The Croatian Serbs insisted on holding a referendum about regional autonomy—charging the new non-Communist government with trampling on their interests. In reality, autonomy would mean transfer to the republic of Serbia.

The movement is organised locally by the Serbian Democratic Party, but it is sponsored by Serbia's rulers, who see the conflict as an extension of its war against the Albanians in the southern area of Kosovo.

Kosovo used to be a relatively autonomous province within Serbia, but now that has changed. Serbia's rulers sought to deflect a country wide strike wave in 1987 and 1988 by scapegoating ethnic Albanians.

This conflict has now reached Intifada type proportions. Reports coming out of Zagreb in September give a flavour:

A movement of strong police forces and more than 40 tanks and

First published November 1990

several police armoured cars halted in the early hours of this morning in Gornia Sipasnica near Kosovska Kamenica, which is inhabited by Albanians. After surrounding the village, eyewitnesses report, a real assault on the population began. A large quantity of tear gas was thrown, local people were harassed, houses were searched and 13 people were detained.'

The Serbian leaders are using the crudest means to maintain their rule. Albanians are being purged from jobs as both managers and workers. Special care is being taken to remove as many Albanians from the mines as possible.

The former leaders of the Communist Party in Kosovo have all been hounded out of office. Former Albanian Communist chief Azem Vllasi, who tried to toe the Serbian line in denouncing 'counter-revolutionary separatists', is now in jail for his pains.

The Albanians have fought back. In February 1989 an occupation of the mines at Trepca was followed by an impressive general strike and widespread street fighting. Another strike by 28,000 workers was staged this October. Some of the strikers had not been paid for six months.

The misery which prompted the promotion of nationalism is still in place. An IMF supported austerity programme has had some successes for Yugoslavia's bosses. Foreign debt has been reduced, and only 15 percent of foreign currency earnings now go to paying off the banks. Inflation has been brought down to near normal levels after peaking at nearly 2,000 percent at the end of last year. However, a wage freeze and factory closure programme have hit workers hard. Industrial production and living standards are both continuing to fall and the federal government called for 15-20 percent spending cuts to fight inflation. The latest trick to make workers suffer for the crisis is to insist they take part of their wages in the form of shares in the enterprises at which they work.

In the absence of a coherent working class response, this misery is sure to fuel further nationalism. Aside from the Croatian events, there are other indicators that Yugoslavia is falling apart. Slovenia has declared its own sovereignty. Macedonia is in turmoil.

Should we worry if Yugoslavia falls apart? Yugoslavia is a historical peculiarity. In no sense is it a nation state. Only around 2 percent of the population consider themselves to be Yugoslavs. But does it constitute a mini-empire in which a dominant nationality oppresses other nationalities? Some of the national relationships clearly do fit this model—for example, the oppression by Serbs of the Albanians and Macedonians.

But what about the rest of the federation? Certainly the Serbs are the most powerful nationality. They far outnumber any other single group, and they hold power out of proportion to their numbers. They account for around two thirds of the officer corps in the army, and a disproportionate amount of the Communist Party. In Croatia, where they constitute just 11 percent of the population, they accounted for 24 percent of Communist Party members in 1978. Over 60 percent of the police in Croatia are thought to be Serbs.

The existence of the multi-national federal structure was designed not to enhance national freedoms, but corresponded to the interests of the bureaucracy in creating economic units suited to the development of the partially market orientated 'self management'—which in effect meant putting the direct burden for the success or failure of enterprises on workers themselves.

Therefore, all other things being equal, the ripping apart of Yugoslavia would not in principle be against the interests of the working class. But the experience of the extension of the struggle to Croatia shows that there is unlikely to be a happy outcome to the break up, as the federation is being threatened almost exclusively from above, not from below.

Croatia is the second richest and second most populous republic in the federation. It will not be easily pushed around. It also has a long tradition of struggle against Serbia—involving reactionary nationalisms on both sides.

Serbian leader Slobodan Milosevic pushed the Croats toward nationalism by launching his campaign for a Greater Serbia. But the Serb minority in Croatia has now been steeled in support for him by the subsequent developments in Croatia, with the rise of a politically reactionary nationalism steeped in a tradition not just of attacking Serbs, but also Jews and Gypsies.

The local leaders of the Serbs claim Franjo Tudjman of the Croatian Democratic Party, who was elected president last April, wants to resurrect the wartime fascist regime which terrorised local Serbs, along with other minorities, and collaborated with the Nazis.

Neither Tudjman nor the Serbian ruler Slobodan Milosevic are about to set up concentration camps, but the process which led to such horrors under the occupation have some parallels with today. The inter-war period was characterised by Croat and Serbian leaders competing for control over different parts of the country and other nationalities.

The Serbs were the most powerful national group, but Croat nationalism failed to effectively challenge them, as it concentrated on resurrecting the most backward cultural traditions. This only divided Serb workers from Croat workers, rather than helping them fight the central state. Tudjman is also now using methods which are at the very least insensitive and tend to throw local Serbs even more into the hands of the Serbian rulers.

The nationalism of the Croat or Slovene rulers may worry Milosevic, but it is not effective in damaging his power, because it fails to link the struggles by workers in those republics with the national struggle.

A break up of Yugoslavia led solely from above could spark the most horrific civil war, with whole communities being uprooted. Serbs form about 11 percent of the population of Croatia. Albanians make up about a fifth of the population of Macedonia. About a third of the population of Bosnia-Hercegovina are Serbs and another fifth are Croats. Muslims in the republic are now organising against repression at the hands of Serbian authorities.

Yugoslavia's rulers have good reasons for wanting to stop short of actually breaking up the federation. The relatively rich Slovenes might earlier have hoped for a special role as the West's foothold in Eastern Europe and thus attract investment. But the collapse of Stalinism has made any Western interest in Slovenia peripheral.

There are real secessionist voices in Macedonia now, but where would they go? The rulers of both Greece and Bulgaria would love to have them, but neither they nor Serbia is going to allow any of the others easy pickings.

In addition, the leaders of the former Communist parties are finding themselves outflanked by even more strident nationalists. For example, an anti-Communist rally in Belgrade on 12 September attracted 20,000 people. Most of the opposition in Belgrade want the return of the Serbian monarchy. Waiting in the wings beyond these organisations is the Serbian Chetnik Party, openly named after the wartime chauvinist organisation which collaborated with the Nazis.

The rulers of Yugoslavia are incapable of untangling the economic and national mess they preside over. The national struggles led from above could turn the situation from its current mess into a nightmare of communalism.

What is the alternative?

Much of the former dissident community has nothing to offer. The supporters of the *Praxis* journal who were at the centre of a search for a real democratic alternative during the 'Zagreb Spring' of 1968-71 are now split. One has joined Milosevic's clique while others are attempting to bridge ethnic divisions by building the Association for a Yugoslav Democratic Initiative.

But a real alternative must be based on joint struggles by workers against both economic hardship and oppression. The opportunity for such fights will continue to arise as all Yugoslavian workers are asked to pay for the crisis. Mobilising such a force depends on the development of a clear political alternative.

Chapter 5

Plunged into chaos

Duncan Blackie

Tanks rolled into the streets of Yugoslavia's capital Belgrade in March in a last ditch bid to save the remnants of the Stalinist regime. Armed units supporting a dozen different causes and authorities vie for power in the republics of Croatia and Bosnia-Hercegovina. Once the most liberal Eastern European regime, Yugoslavia is now becoming one of the most volatile.

Two events sparked the latest chaos. One was a clash between units in the army and local police in the town of Pakrac in Croatia. The surrounding self proclaimed autonomous region of Krajina is mostly Serbian, and the Serbian leadership have been keen to deploy the army against the Croats.

The Serbian leaders have long been in conflict with the leaders of Croatia and other republics such as Slovenia. Differing economic priorities and the promotion of chauvinism in both republics fuelled these tensions.

But the tension became unbearable by the end of last year after the Croats elected an anti-Communist president, Franjo Tudjman, and December elections returned Slobodan Milosevic as president in Serbia. Milosevic heads the Serbian Socialist Party, the old Communist Party in disguise, and has distinguished himself through his promotion of a vicious anti-Albanian campaign. However, the maturing of the chauvinist campaign has led to the second element of emergency.

Milosevic kept his popularity for a long period by generating a wave of Serbian chauvinism and proclaiming Albanian separatists and Croatian expansionists the real enemy.

The Serbian leadership ran back towards classic Stalinism while other East European rulers ran from it. All the press and media in Serbia were subordinated to the party, which made them a particular target when the storm broke. But this strategy could only *disguise* the

First published April 1991

economic pain suffered by most of his followers, not cure it.

Yugoslavia has stepped back from the catastrophic hyper-inflation of two years ago, but at a price. Devaluation and a currency link with the German mark stabilised the currency but has smashed industrial output. In January of this year it was 18.2 percent down on the year before. This drastic figure masks even starker regional falls. Production in the impoverished southern regions of Kosovo and Montenegro has fallen by 36.5 percent and 23.9 percent respectively. Even in relatively prosperous Croatia, output has fallen by 22.9 percent over the last year.

The division of powers between Yugoslavia's republican leaders allowed some of them to get round these problems, but only at the cost of prolonging and exacerbating the crisis.

Workers have taken repeated action to stave off these attacks. Just before the latest crisis broke, thousands of Serbian workers protested outside the Republic Assembly building in Belgrade and forced the government to give them months of back pay. A near general strike by metal and textile workers was averted when they were finally paid in a similar incident.

However, when the dam finally burst, discontent channelled neither into straightforward workers' struggles or towards continuing support for Milosevic. The hundreds of thousands thronging Belgrade's streets now supported a new set of leaders, and were bent on removing the old rulers.

The leaders and the masses' aspirations are mixed. Some are vaguely social democratic. Many more have hazy notions of returning to what they imagine was an ethnically balanced Yugoslavia in Tito's days.

The majority are for now, however, standing behind Vuk Draskovic, the leader of the Serbian Renewal Movement. Draskovic is firmly anti-Communist, untainted as Milosevic is by the past. But he is also a pure Serbian reactionary, someone who wanted to go even further than the Communists in the suppression of the Albanians.

This situation is full of the most tense contradictions. Chauvinism runs incredibly deep. It is testament to Milosevic's campaign, and the lack of any socialist or even consistently liberal alternative, that virtually every significant political player has been won to some form of chauvinism.

But against this depressing side must be set the contradictions in the chauvinists' programmes. The most obvious is that Milosevic has already carried most of them out. The opposition have no new economic ideas, and their nationalism also looks decidedly tawdry. The predominantly ethnic Albanian province of Kosovo is already under martial law.

Chauvinism has been rampant for four years, but it could now be challenged by a crisis of its own making. The Serbian Socialist Party's use of troops—Serb against Serb—has fractured the enchanted glass of nationalism. Meanwhile senior army officers have closed in behind a party formed by Milosevic's wife, Mirjana, the League of Communists-Movement for Yugoslavia (SK-PJ), 'the best armed party'. Rumours and rhetoric make it difficult to assess the real situation, but there are strong indications that all the hardware is already in place for an enormous battle. The Croatian Democratic Community (HDZ) has been accused of creating units ready for a rising. HDZ members have already seen action. They ignored a weapons amnesty, and in late January 450 of them surrounded an army barracks in Virovitica. Franjo Tudjman claims the army seized 200,000 pieces of light armoury from militias in the republic at the end of last year, including rifles, machine guns, mortars and anti-tank guns. The official news agency claims that Hungary has verified claims that over 10,000 Kalashnikovs were illegally imported from that country. Guns worth DM2.9 million are said to have been imported from Panama. Slovenian police claim to have seized over 5,500 illegal weapons last year, twice their usual haul. On the other side the Serbian Renewal Movement calls for the setting up of a purely Serbian army. Elsewhere, the Internal Macedonian Revolutionary Organisation-Democratic Party for Macedonian Unity (VMRO-DPMNE), the local party with the most deputies, calls for the ejection of the army from Macedonia.

The Yugoslavian crisis is not some sordid little local battle, separate from the rest of the New World Order—it *is* the New World Order.

Two Balkan wars and then the First World War were fought over its land as the country was pieced together from three declining empires. The Second World War was particularly bloody as half a dozen different powers scrapped over its territory. Two factors stabilised Yugoslavia in the post-war period. Firstly, economic growth gave the impression that the country's blood soaked history could be overcome. Secondly, Yugoslavia was a Cold War dead zone. It was supposed to be a stable linchpin in the European order. As long as Yugoslavia remained intact it had the effect of freezing over the territorial ambitions of many other states. Now it is falling apart.

As the *Wall Street Journal* reported:

Six of Yugoslavia's seven neighbours have a territorial claim against it, and some, such as Bulgaria, might press harder if Yugoslavia lacked any central authority. Such claims could require intervention by other countries to preserve current borders. And an upheaval in Yugoslavia could inflame the minority disputes in most of Eastern Europe—and in Western Europe, too.

No country in Europe better illustrates the stark alternatives posed by capitalism in crisis. Old rulers, and even old borders, are being torn up. Croat, Serb and Albanian workers are all suffering from the crisis. Their only objective interests lie in fighting together.

But the tragedy of Yugoslavia is that the opposition movement has itself been Balkanised. Even in the case of the movement which came closest to fighting for a real alternative—that of the Croatian democratic movement in the early 1970s—leadership was ceded to local bureaucrats who made their peace with the Stalinists at the earliest opportunity.

Today the anguished masses of all the republics are again being led by parties which can offer them nothing. This historic failure of the working class to develop its own movements and thereby overcome national divisions is now about to plunge Yugoslavia into chaos.

This is the future

'The time will come when people actually get fed up with killing each other.' This crassest of judgements on the civil war in Yugoslavia came from British home secretary Douglas Hurd. In its sheer stupidity it crowned international efforts to resolve a situation which is running out of everyone's control. The desperation of Yugoslavia's slide into chaos is shown by the Beirut type frequency with which ceasefires are declared and ignored.

The horror should not be underestimated. Hundreds have already died in fighting, first between Slovenia and the federal army, and then, on a much more vicious basis, between Croatian units and what is now a Serbian army. On the surface, the situation is a nightmarish challenge to anyone who believes human progress is possible. Villages which have been home for centuries to both Croats and Serbs are now rent apart.

Below the surface, however, the civil war is a concentrated brew of the desperation which exists in a crisis ridden world from Moscow to New York.

How does this carnage sit with the era of peace and prosperity which was supposedly opened up by the fall of the Berlin Wall and US victory in the Gulf? The supporters of the New World Order have this down as a blemish caused by, in the words of one of Bush's aides this spring, 'a bunch of slugs and thugs down in Belgrade'.

But every Western ruler realises that the Yugoslavian tragedy is also a challenge to which they have no real answers. At the very least, they realise that the way in which economic crisis has fuelled the revival of old ethnic tensions can very soon become generalised across the rest of Eastern Europe, and even into Western Europe. Spain's rulers now talk about the 'Croatian effect' in Catalonia and the Basque Country.

Some of the Western powers see opportunities to intervene in their own interests. The German ruling class would love to take its place

First published October 1991

in the New World Order by direct intervention, if it thought they could get away with it. It does not, so one moment Chancellor Kohl backs a 'peacekeeping force', and the next explains that the constitution precludes it being made up of Germans. Lord Carrington, sent by the EC to oversee a peace process, says he can't start work until peace has broken out.

The dangers of intervention for the ruling class are plain to see. EC observers have already learned that they cannot even just watch the shooting without running the risk of getting shot themselves. Some have talked of appointing bodyguards to guard the observers. But if the bodyguards become involved in forfeits, then the pressure will be on for greater forces, and so on.

The paralysis of the Western governments stems from the fact that Yugoslavia is not a leftover of a past era, some cauldron of irrational Eastern nationalism or the result of Stalinists still managing to hold onto the last vestiges of power in Belgrade. This is the future.

The mess that exists is at least partly the creation of those European and North American governments who now want to step in and sort it out. The market has been increasingly applied in Yugoslavia ever since state capitalist development ran out of steam in the mid- to late 1960s. Yugoslavia has been progressively drawn into the world system and has become an example of what the market can offer a relatively weak economy. Some $20 billion worth of debt was run up by the early 1980s. Then the IMF arrived to work its wonders. The result was widescale closures, unemployment, wage cuts and the impoverishment of millions of people.

The economic divisions between the north and south of the country have been exacerbated by the market. Every region has suffered in the past decade, but not all to the same extent. Slovenian and Croatian manufacturing plants have looked attractive to Western investors. Not so the poor, basic industries of the south. Under the period of Western intervention, the income differentials between rich and poor have widened enormously, so that Slovenes are on average six times better off than the mainly Albanian inhabitants of Kosovo.

The victims of this assault—coordinated between privileged bureaucrats in Belgrade and privileged bureaucrats in the boardrooms of Western banks—have fought back. Successive waves of strikes have rolled over the country since the mid-1980s.

Croat, Serb, Slovene and Albanian workers have all fought separately and sometimes together to alleviate the economic agony. They fought so successfully that the ruling elite floundered between one failed 'solution' and the next. They had to chop and change between more of the market, more central planning, this promise, that loan, in order to survive. None of it worked.

Then each of the national groups which made up the Yugoslavian ruling class discovered that it was possible to deflect the anger through nationalism. This was first tried out successfully by Serbian leader Slobodan Milosevic in his campaign against the Albanians from 1987 onwards. All those European rulers who now claim to have the national interests of the Croats at heart showed no such concern over repeated assaults on the Albanians.

By last spring the leaders of every republic had decided they needed the same tactics. Slovenes and Croats were told that their problems were the fault of 'backward' Serbs whose dependence on federal funds was to blame for economic decline. Former Communist Party bosses changed the names of their parties, renounced or hid their past as privileged members of a united Yugoslavian ruling class, and hoisted nationalist banners over themselves. In this way they all succeeded in building mass movements which could undercut the struggles for real change.

This is not to say that the class struggle was just stopped in its tracks as everyone was duped by the lies about other nationalities. But it did create a situation in which two alternative routes of struggle were on offer.

This was shown most clearly in Belgrade in April of this year, when no less than three movements rocked the capital. Students took to the streets to demand democracy and the end of the Serbian Socialist Party, Milosevic's thinly disguised party of old bureaucrats. But, directionless, this movement was soon taken over and subverted by ultra-nationalists to the right of even Milosevic, who called for the expulsion of all non-Serbs from Serbia. No sooner was this done, however, than 700,000 workers went on strike in Serbia—against the Serbian leaders—demanding wages which had been held up for months.

Meanwhile the objective base of all the tensions, the economic crisis, was becoming deeper still. The country's leadership had attempted to solve a chronic inflationary problem by tying the Yugoslavian currency to the German mark. The result was to subject the economy to the same level of pressures as in Poland or East Germany, and 40 percent of manufacturing output was wiped out.

As quickly as the nationalist rhetoric was increased, the economic misery deepened. Now the nationalist leaders took the only logical step possible for them—if nationalist rhetoric had not snuffed out class antagonism, then action was needed. The road to war was thus opened up by the acute economic crisis exacerbated at every turn by the market.

Such agony has been imposed on ordinary people that many Serbs now hark back to the pre-war tradition of the Chetniks—Serbian supremacists. Similarly, many Croats now claim the legacy of the Ustashe—Second World War Croatian fascists. Even now most Serbs and Croats are neither of these things—they are confused and desperate for any solution—but enough of them exist to fuel the claims and prejudices on each opposing side.

Socialists have to respond to this situation by arguing for equal rights for all nationalities. That means opposing the invasion of Croatia and supporting its right to split away if it wants. Croats cannot be equal with Serbs if they are forced into an unequal union. On the other hand, the leaders of Croatia offer no alternative. Instead of weakening Milosevic by encouraging Serbian workers to continue their fightback against the bureaucrats in Belgrade, their nationalism has undermined even the fight for national independence. Tudjman directed his fire first and foremost on Serbs who have lived in Croatia for centuries. Operations were carried out at the end of last year and the start of this to purge the police and territorial defence of all Serbs. An atmosphere of fear was created in which the claims by Milosevic that army intervention was needed to stop a repeat of the Second World War pogroms got a real hearing among Croatia's Serbs.

The *Financial Times* has even been able to find a former adviser to Tudjman who admitted:

> We should have politically disarmed the Serbs in Croatia by promising them cultural autonomy and rights... We left it too late. Last year's election campaign by the Christian Democratic Union was won on a Croatian nationalist platform. Tudjman insisted that all Serbs take an oath of loyalty to the Croatian state. This played into the hands of Serbian nationalists and Slobodan Milosevic, who keeps accusing us of being fascists.

Yugoslavia has all the potential of ending in real barbarism—in the sense of the ruination of all contending parties. No Western power can hope to reap easy gains from the situation. Even the Serbian leaders cannot hope for a military solution—beyond the Serbian populated margins of Croatia, they are heading for a quagmire in which their superior arms will be of little use. The Serbian and Croatian leaders can offer nothing more than economic misery and pogroms.

The crisis rolls on across the country, with Albanians now suffering renewed persecution in Macedonia. Macedonia itself is now being eyed up by both Greek and Bulgarian rulers. In Slovenia, new scapegoats have emerged—Gypsies, who were physically excluded from polling booths in the local elections.

There should be despair at Yugoslavia—despair that after experimentation by both state and market capitalism, nothing is left but a horrible rerun of all the rival ambitions and national tensions of both world wars.

There are, however, some chinks of light. There is mass desertion from the army by Serbian conscripts, as well as those of other nationalities. Movements of conscripts' mothers calling for the return of their sons have taken off in both Zagreb and Belgrade.

Perhaps even more significantly, the *Financial Times* reported that a 'revolt by several hundred draftees in the small town of Velika Plana, 1,000km east of the Serbian capital, earlier this week was clear proof that the army's role in the undeclared civil war is far from universally supported.'

Whether such movements take off, and fuse with the recent traditions of class struggle, or whether they are smothered once more by nationalism, the alternatives are clear: a movement from below which can identify and build around common grievances across the nationalities; or a variety of solutions from above which, whether they come from Belgrade, Zagreb or Brussels, can only end in more misery.

Chapter 7

The road to hell

Duncan Blackie

Nine years short of the 21st century a corner of Europe once again rings to the battle cries of the 19th century. The collapse of Yugoslavia into civil war has confounded explanation from those—on both left and right—who have held Yugoslavia to be a 'miracle' of the market, 'self managed socialism' or a 'third road' alternative to Stalinism and Western market capitalism. Every feature of the most hopeless areas of the world is in place. By the autumn of 1991 the country was rent between warlords, the economy in freefall.

The scale of the crisis needs little elaboration. Thousands were dead within the first weeks of full scale armed encounters between Serbian and Croatian forces. Thousands have been uprooted, forced out of their jobs and homes. Many hundreds of thousands could end up homeless or dead because of the battle that started to rage in the summer of 1991. And the crisis does not stop at the federal borders. The mangled, distorted development of capitalism in the region will make sure that shockwaves spread from Yugoslavia, scarcely losing their power as they roll across half a continent.

Those in power saw the danger as US, Russian and European Community leaders rushed to make ineffectual interventions. George Bush's aides described the competing Yugoslav leaders as 'slugs' and 'thugs' who were getting in the way of the New World Order.[1] John Major at first declared that 'the first prize is to hold the federation together',[2] but by September his foreign secretary, Douglas Hurd, could only hope that 'the time will come when people actually get fed up with killing each other'.[3] They live scared that Yugoslavia, so long held to be an exception, a testing ground for 'reform Communism', will now become a model in a different sense: a spark which will make a bonfire of all their hopes for Eastern Europe.

The country is living proof that even in an industrialised country

First published in an extended version winter 1991

the market is capable of introducing Third World style horrors. It is also an example of the way in which the agony of economic decline can feed into and reproduce separate national aspirations and hatreds which the world's rulers have successively hoped to contain after both world wars, and now under the New World Order. As the country falls apart all the major powers are caught between the temptation to intervene to slice off the more prosperous region, and the horrifying prospect of becoming embroiled in a war of a different order of magnitude to that in Ireland. Smaller powers could get drawn into border disputes. How long will Romania and Albania stay out of the fray? How long until Serbia, Bulgaria and Greece are once more embroiled in a fight for Macedonia?

Seen in this way, the crisis is simple. It represents an all round catastrophe of the first order, with innumerable ethnic groups and states fighting each other. For many critics this seems obvious enough—we are dealing with the Balkans. Three regional wars and the First World War started here. Civil wars raged for a whole decade during and after the Second World War. Here is a territory with a history of strife, where politicians have been naive enough in the past to expect people of different religious, ethnic and national backgrounds to live in peace. A grim truth, however, is hidden beneath this excuse. Yugoslavia has been to the market. The agencies which now aim to revive the East European economies have been experimenting in Yugoslavia for over 20 years.

The national question

Most discussions of the national question in Yugoslavia start by concentrating on the complications which allegedly flow from the sheer number of different groups involved: two scripts, six republics, 22 nationalities and so on. But the murderous nature of nationalism today does not spring from such cultural diversity, but from more direct political and economic sources which have fed into national channels. The main fault lines are relatively easy to trace.

Serbs and Croats are both descendants of the Slavic tribes who first settled in the area of northern Yugoslavia in the 7th century. For the 800 years until 1914 Croats lived under the domination of Austria and for 500 years until the 19th century most Serbs lived under Turkish rule.[4] The nature of these empires left an indelible mark on the region. The weakness of the empires implanted an economic and social backwardness on the Balkans which was later to be perpetuated by French, British and Russian intervention. This imperial weakness also gave a particularity to the development of nationalism. While in Western Europe economic development impelled the *unification* of territories, the arrested development of the Balkans and the practice of both the Austro-Hungarian and Ottoman empires of granting limited autonomy to different regions ensured that nationalism was bound to be localised.[5]

Thus peoples, like the Serbs and the Croats, who came from such similar backgrounds preserved distinct identities. However, throughout most of this long epoch Serbs who had fled north from the Ottoman Empire lived alongside Croats without friction. As the Ottoman Empire weakened, its grip over Serbia progressively slackened, with the state gaining *de facto* independence under rural dynasties in the early 19th century, and then official independence in 1878. At the same time Austria-Hungary seized Bosnia. But the fate of the Serbian state was still overwhelmingly determined from outside. Britain and Russia saw it as a useful weapon against both the Ottoman and the Austro-Hungarian empires. Therefore the region fell into war three times as the Ottoman Empire declined, the first leading to the independence of Serbia, followed by two armed grabs for land before the outbreak of the First World War. Middling sized countries were caught between struggling for liberation from the Great Powers and carving out their own territory at the expense of each other and the smallest Balkan nationalities.

The development of the Balkans also shaped the other nationalities. Slovenes, like Croats, lived under the Austro-Hungarian Empire, with a large degree of autonomy. The Slovene language is distinct from Serbo-Croat, and the territory's position, set back from the shifting front line between Ottoman and Austro-Hungarian empires, left the area relatively homogenous.[6] Perhaps the most distinct group within Yugoslavia is the Albanian speaking population. They are not descended from the Slavic tribes, and have a distinct history and culture. Most are Muslims, although many are Catholic. They too fought against the Ottomans, standing alongside Serbs at the Battle of Kosovo. But, as we will see, the position and history of the Albanian speaking population were to put them at a special disadvantage both before and after the Second World War.

Macedonians, in the extreme south of Yugoslavia, have a distinct language and culture. But this nationality has also been shaped by events across the whole region. Wedged between Serbia, Greece and

Bulgaria, the territory has been fought over repeatedly, grabbed by all the parties and redivided. The Treaty of San Stefano in 1878 gave it to Bulgaria, but it was then separated from Bulgaria at the Treaty of Berlin later the same year. A Macedonian rising in 1903 was crushed by Turkey, and the next year Serbian guerillas started raids into the territory. Today the existence of a Macedonian nationality is officially denied in Greece, and one of the canons of Serbian chauvinism is that the Macedonians are 'South Serbs'.

Bosnia-Hercegovina, in the centre of Yugoslavia, is populated today by Serbs, Croats and Muslims. The Muslims of this area are defined as a separate nationality. They too are Slavic, and speak Serbo-Croat, but many of them are the descendants of a people who converted to the Bogumil Christian sect in the 15th century. After the area was taken over by the Ottomans, they converted wholesale to Islam.[7] In Montenegro, to the south of Serbia, an independent state had existed since the 15th century and proved impenetrable to Venetian and then Ottoman intervention. This distinct history gave rise to the peculiar national identity of Montenegrins. They have the same language as Serbs, and yet the history of independence at once gives rise to claims of being a separate nation, and of being a special part of the Serbian nation. In the battles of the late 1980s Serbian nationalists played on this latter sentiment to enlist Montenegrins alongside them against other nationalities.

The last major national grouping is the Hungarians who make up about a fifth of the Vojvodina area of Serbia. This was a part of the Austro-Hungarian Empire, and largely Hungarian populated in the 19th century. But Serbian immigration was encouraged in order to create a buffer zone against the Ottomans, which was given autonomy briefly in the second half of the 19th century. In the post-war period it was an autonomous province of the Serbian republic.

The Kingdom of Serbs, Croats and Slovenes was carved out at the end of the First World War from these remnants of the Ottoman and Austro-Hungarian empires. The Western powers, especially the British, sponsored the creation of the state as an extension of the Serbian kingdom, which they calculated had served their interests well. However, the new state was also welcomed by Croat and Slovene landlords. The Croat landlords had relied on the Austro-Hungarian Empire to quell peasant resistance. Now they faced a general rising and welcomed support from the only force that could now save them—the Serbian army. The 'upper class' were 'pleading for the entry of the

Serbian army into Croatia-Slovenia'.[8] Similarly the Slovene landlords preferred to take their territory as a whole into the new kingdom, rather than risk partition between Austria and Italy.[9]

Nevertheless, the oppression of Croats was built into the new state. High office went to Serbs, and the Latin script used by the Croats was banned. Bands of Serbian chauvinists, the Chetniks, were given a free rein to terrorise other nationalities in mixed areas such as Bosnia-Hercegovina. Economic crisis led to King Alexander assuming dictatorial power in 1929 when the country was renamed Yugoslavia. Two distinctive strands of Croatian nationalism developed in this period. One, the Ustashe, attracting mainly students, looked to fascism. A much broader movement for greater autonomy, however, developed among the peasantry. This was represented by the Peasant Party, which affiliated to the Profintern in 1924-25. It argued for Croatian rights, but also set its face against collaborating with foreign powers who wished to exploit the situation for their own ends.

With the start of the Second World War and the annexation of the country by the Axis powers in 1941, oppressions and divisions which had been sponsored by the leaders and supporters of pre-war Yugoslavia (notably the British) were easily switched over and put to good use by the Axis powers. Germany, Italy, Hungary, Albania and Bulgaria all took territories and set up collaborationist regimes in others. Pride of place went to the Independent State of Croatia. Germany and Italy provided the state's might, but the dirtiest work was carried out by the Ustashe. Jews were exterminated on a mass basis, and 98 percent of the Gypsy population was wiped out.[10] For Serbs in Croatia, massacres were followed by offers of clemency if they converted to Catholicism.

Meanwhile, two opposition movements were building up. The first, the Chetniks, consisted of Serbian officers who balked at the surrender to Germany. They fell under the leadership of the pro-Allied monarchist General Mihailovic, who looked to the pre-war traditions of Serbian supremacy. The other group, the partisans, was led by the Communist Party and aimed at liberating and reuniting the country. Two factors were to decide that the partisans came out on top. The first was the vacillation of Mihailovic, who repeatedly approached Germany with deals. The second was that the partisans realised that whoever could unite the warring nationalities would come out on top. Their prowess won the support of Britain away from Mihailovic. Churchill demanded, 'Find out who was killing the most Germans and suggest means by which [to] help them kill more'.[11]

Tito's achievement in building a movement which united Serbs, Slovenes, Croats, Macedonians and others was impressive. Not only did it win the war of liberation, it also left indelible marks on the post-war state. One of these was the creation of the Macedonian republic. Without making this concession to the Macedonians the southern frontier would have been impossible to hold. The second was the creation of a state in which the three decades of systematic inequality between Serbs and Croats were decisively overcome. This is why the chauvinist labels of today have to be dredged up from *before* 1945; neither the Croats nor the Serbs can claim, with the Albanians, to have suffered oppression since the Second World War.

Economically, the Croats have done better than the average for Yugoslavia. They speak Serbo-Croat,[12] one of the three official languages of state (along with Macedonian and Slovene) and the only official language of the army. Historically they have been well represented among almost all elite groups. The table below, which shows the representation of various nationalities in the ruling circles of their respective areas, demonstrates the stark dissimilarity with the Albanians:[13]

Elite sectors (representation of host nationalities in each republic)		
	Percentage of total pop	Percentage of total elite
Croats in Croatia	79.4	79.8
Muslims in Bosnia-Hercegovina	39.6	31.1
Hungarians in Vojvodina	21.7	14.7
Albanians in Kosovo	73.7	34.5

The alleged suppression of the Catholic church at the hands of the Communists, while the Orthodox was tolerated, is often used as an example of national oppression. Catholic Cardinal Stepinac was jailed at the end of the Second World War, for example. This explanation, however, leaves out of account the fact that the Catholic church had become virtually a wing of the fascist state which the partisans overthrew. A number of Orthodox collaborators were also jailed at the end of the war.[14]

The bizarre claim is even made that the Croats have been *economically* oppressed. This usually focuses on two claims. The first is that, after the dismantling of much federal and republican financial control

(42.5 percent of investment in 1863 to 8.8 percent in 1971), control over finances reverted in large part to the banks, which were all based in Belgrade. This, however, did not stop Croatia being more prosperous than Serbia. Secondly, it is said, Croats have suffered by having to pay more taxes on their more successful enterprises![15]

The campaign against the Albanians

'What we are discussing here can no longer be called politics—it is a question of our fatherland,' Serbian party boss Slobodan Milosevic told a party meeting in 1987.[16] He was fresh from a huge rally of Serbs at Kosovo Polje in which he evoked the medieval struggles against the Ottomans in order to convince Serbian workers that their main problem was the threat posed by local ethnic Albanians. But Kosovo Polje was the site of a battle in 1389 against the Ottomans in which the Albanians fought *alongside* the Serbs! Yet Milosevic got a rapturous reception. He got a hearing because the unresolved agony of ordinary Serbs could find no other outlet.

If there is a people in Yugoslavia which has suffered national oppression since the Second World War, then it is the Albanians who make up over 80 percent of the population of Kosovo. The Albania drawn by the great powers on the map in 1913 included only a part of those lands inhabited by Albanians. The area that is now Kosovo and part of Macedonia was given to the Serbs in 1913 as recompense for their efforts in the Balkan Wars. Between the wars Kosovo was treated as conquered territory, with Serbs given sponsorship and free land as encouragement to go and settle those lands overrun by the Serbian armies in 1912-13. Between the wars 40,000 Orthodox slavs moved to Kosovo. Half a million Albanians were forced out.[17]

Even after the post-war settlement, which, as we shall see, marked a departure from the pre-war set up in many respects, the Albanians still had an unequal position. Whereas Croats, Serbs, Slovenes and others are officially deemed 'nations' and therefore were given their own republics with a degree of autonomy from the centre, the Albanians were declared a 'nationality'. Their state, it was argued, was over the border in Albania proper—regardless of the fact that the most terrible conceivable political crime in Yugoslavia was for an Albanian to publicly identify with Albania.

Kosovo is the poorest corner of Europe. Repeated claims were made about how it too was experiencing an economic miracle; 'a unique example of socio-economic development'.[18] Yet it has continually fallen behind the rest of Yugoslavia. In 1954 per capita income was 48 percent of the Yugoslav average. By 1975 it was 33 percent. The fundamental problem was that the tinkering represented by central assistance was no match for the economic pull of the market. Industrial labour productivity was only 70 percent of the national average. The rate of capital accumulation was less than one half of the national average.[19] So by 1988 75 percent of the population depended on benefits, real unemployment ran at about 50 percent and over 70 percent of women were illiterate.[20]

The region experienced a brief liberalisation after the fall of Rankovic in 1966, and greater autonomy under the 1974 constitution. But when students led a mass movement for real autonomy in 1968, they were crushed. Revolt blew up again in 1981. On 11 March 1981 students marched through Pristina demanding better conditions. They were attacked by the police. On 26 March more demonstrations took place and, fittingly, the local stage of the all Yugoslav youth relay race was broken up.[21]

In the mid- and late 1980s the Albanians were to be subjected to even worse treatment as party bosses thrashed around for solutions to their chronic problems. Others had already taken up the campaign. In 1986 right wingers inside and outside the party, intellectuals, the Orthodox church and a motley collection around the Kosovo Committee produced a petition, the Memorandum, accusing the party and state leadership of high treason for betrayal of the Serbs. Its authors claimed the Albanians wanted a 'bourgeois society governed by a profascist right wing regime'.

The Serbian Communist Party had been increasingly polarised between two strategies. One group wished to apply some of the openness being displayed in Slovenia, in the hope that a more liberal regime might be able to shrug off some of the discontent. The other faction, headed by Slobodan Milosevic and a group of hard nosed pragmatists who had risen through the machine in the early 1980s, preferred a different strategy. They aimed for an authoritarian solution which would both roll back the autonomy given to the provinces and the republics and, through flattening workers' resistance with repression and nationalism, lay the basis for the economic recovery of Yugoslavia.

In 1987 Milosevic and his coterie had gained decisive control of the Belgrade party. They quickly rushed to the head of the Serbian nationalist movement and led it on. The official media waged a ridiculous, but effective, campaign of lies about alleged atrocities in Kosovo, including inventions about the rape of Serb women and Albanian plots to overrun the place through sheer effort of breeding. Laws were changed to effectively reinstate the Serb population as colonisers. Land was not to be sold to Albanians. Serb only factories were built. Serb villages threw out Albanian inhabitants. The media cried, 'Let's go, brothers and sisters, to attack Kosovo'.[22] Serbian leaders claimed a 'genocide' was taking place in the very 'cradle of the nation'—witness the decline in the Kosovo Serbian population. True, people did leave if they could—everyone did, as unemployment was 50 percent as early as 1970. Yet, while hundreds of young Albanians have been killed by Serbian forces in the last two years, not one Albanian 'terrorist' has succeeded in killing a single Serb.[23]

Milosevic organised mass rallies in Serbia, Kosovo and Vojvodina, terrorising the Albanians and using the power of mass mobilisation both to wed Serbian workers to chauvinism and also to discipline other sections of the bureaucracy. This way Milosevic, the individual then most responsible for the chronic state of the biggest slice of the Yugoslav economy, managed to amass a tremendous personal following.

When it became obvious that Milosevic aimed to topple the government in Vojvodina and Montenegro as well as Kosovo, the rest of Yugoslavia's leadership suddenly woke up to the dangers of the situation. The Vojvodina government in Novi Sad was quickly toppled by a combination of official pressure and mass mobilisation. Then the bandwagon moved on to Montenegro. The events here, however, must have let even Milosevic know that he was playing with fire. True, the nationalists eventually took the heads of the Montenegrin government. But along the way they came close to losing the initiative to workers fighting in their own interests.

The events revealed that *two* torrents of bitterness were running through Serbia—that generated by the nationalists and a realisation among workers that no amount of chauvinist rallies would improve their desperate economic plight. Fifty eight percent of Belgrade workers did not earn enough to satisfy their basic needs at the time.[24] The *Financial Times* reported:

> Emboldened by the power of popular protest, Yugoslavs have shifted the focus of their three month street campaign from nationalist demands to complaints over their country's economic disarray... During last week's protests in Novi Sad, the Vojvodina capital, and in Montenegro, the wrath of the demonstrators was directed at the local

Communist leaderships... The Titograd demonstration was sparked off by workers at the Titex factory who can no longer tolerate the struggle for survival on wages of 100,000 dinars (about £20) a month. But the demonstrators appeared to have had little time for the small group of Serbian nationalist agitators who were demanding the blood of Albanians.[25]

Everywhere Milosevic's nationalist card was raising the stakes, and as much as other party bosses admired and tried to emulate it, they were also set against him. The Croatian and Slovene bosses had no time for the Albanians, but they knew an unconditionally triumphant Milosevic would leave them in a weaker position. Meanwhile, the resistance of the Albanians themselves was an enormous drain on Serbia—the policing of Kosovo alone soaked up 22 percent of the republic's funds by the start of the 1990s.[26] Even this effort has not succeeded in breaking resistance.

In November 1988 the Serbian *and* federal authorities had arranged for Kosovo president Kaqusha Jashari and her successor, Azem Vllasi, to resign. The move, however, met stiff resistance. Miners set out to march 70 kilometres to Pristina. They joined a half million strong demonstration (Kosovo has a population of just over two million). They failed to stop the resignations, but laid the basis for the general strike which was launched at the start of 1989 against the Serbian clampdown. About 1,300 lead and zinc miners at the Trepca complex occupied their pits and staged a hunger strike for eight days. By the strike's end 180 were in hospital, many in intensive care. Significantly, the first group of workers to send solidarity greetings were the miners of Slovenia.[27]

The miners secured the resignation of three hated Serbian imposed officials, but after the staging of mass rallies in Serbia they were reinstated and arrests were made of the strike activists. Vllasi was sentenced to 14 months in jail in early 1990. Direct rule was imposed in late 1990. Now the leaders of other republics felt compelled to act. Croat and Slovene militias were withdrawn from Kosovo.

By now a new phase of the crisis was developing, in which the plummeting economy not only set Serbs against the oppressed Albanians, but was eventually to prove capable of generating such bitterness that non-oppressed nations such as the Croats would find themselves at war.

The second fracture: Serbs and Croats

At the end of the 1980s there appeared, from the outside, to be a respite. The years 1988 and 1989 were known for chronic inflation, reaching 2,500 percent a year at one point. However, this crisis seemed to have passed after a series of measures, including the introduction of the *new* new dinar, linked to the German mark. At the start of April 1990 an inflation rate of minus 1.5 percent was registered.[28]

In Yugoslavia itself these measures were disastrous. In part, the new currency merely disguised a real inflation felt by workers. 'From being one of the cheapest countries in Europe, Yugoslavia became one of the most expensive overnight'.[29] In 1987 the republics of Kosovo, Macedonia and Montenegro had all declared themselves bankrupt. By the start of 1990 even in the most prosperous republic of Slovenia 40 percent of enterprises were running at a loss.[30] The strike wave continued. Output fell by 23 percent in 1990 and then by another 21 percent in the first five months of 1991. There are no more recent figures for the federal economy— it ceased to exist at some point in the summer of 1991, victim of the political crisis which the ailing economy had itself created.[31]

We have seen how the economic crisis tended to draw the different republics apart, in order to protect their own interests. Now the leaders of every republic also responded to the precipitous crisis by raising nationalism to new levels in order to draw away working class anger. Collectively, the Yugoslavian ruling class set off a chain of events that was to lead to the meltdown of 1991.

For two years, first in Serbia, then elsewhere, the Communist bosses sponsored an increase in nationalism in order to divert workers from their struggles. But having done this, and failing at the same time to improve economic conditions at all, the controlled, manipulated movement which was launched in 1987 started to take on a life of its own. Everywhere nationalists more sincere than the party bosses started to organise. Everywhere the demand was for an end to Communism. Now lifelong Communist bosses pretended to turn away from their responsibility for the mess.

In Slovenia, Milan Kucan took his section of the party out of the Federal League of Communists and declared that elections would be held. The opposition DEMOS coalition won these on 8 April 1990 and increasingly moved to a position of demanding secession from the federation as a precondition to any talk over a future Yugoslavia.

Kucan himself managed to hold on as president. Now this long time ally of the rest of the Yugoslavian Communist leadership, and long standing fan of Margaret Thatcher, renamed his party the Slovene Communist Party-Party of Democratic Renewal. Other Communist leaders also spruced up their image. The Socialist Party of Serbia was miraculously born out of the merger of the Communists with other front organisations. In Croatia the Communists amended their name to the Communist Party-Party for Democratic Change and declared elections, but they could not hold on to office. On 22 April the Croatian elections were won by the Croatian Democratic Union (HDZ).

The HDZ is led by ex-Communist Franjo Tudjman, one of Tito's henchmen, a colonel in the general staff and the bureaucrat in charge of 'cadre questions' in the army.[32] In the summer of 1990 the HDZ announced that federal authority over Croatia was to end. In December, elections were held in Serbia, which were won by the former Communist Party. On 22 December the Croatian parliament adopted a new constitution with the right to secede and the next day a plebiscite in Slovenia resulted in a 90 percent majority in favour of secession. Meanwhile, the political consequences of the economic crisis were feeding back to wreck the economy completely. In the spring of 1990 the Serbian leadership declared an economic blockade of Slovenia. By the end of the year both the northern republics were withholding their contributions to the federal budget, arguing it was not fair to give so much to an army which was likely to be used against them.

By the start of 1991 there was no longer a Yugoslav economy to argue over. In January the republics of Croatia, Macedonia, Montenegro and Serbia all printed their own stocks of money. The Serbian leaders hoped that the $1.6 billion worth of notes which they secretly printed might shut Serbian workers up for a while.[33] In February negotiations over a new federal structure broke down. By now, however, a guerilla struggle had already started up in Croatia between the republican authorities and local Serbs. The Serbs made up 12 percent of the population of Croatia at the last census. Some lived in mainly Serb villages, many more in mixed settlements. They and their ancestors had lived and worked with Croats for centuries. In many cases it would be impossible to say who was the more established. Now Milosevic sought to turn these Serbs into a fifth column by appealing to them as the front line of the Serbian nation, who stood to be wiped out if Croatian nationalism was not beaten. Under his sponsorship the Serbian Democratic Party had been set up in February 1990 and in July the Serbian National Council declared autonomy for Serbs. He would have had little success, were it not for events taking place in Croatia which revived memories of the brief but bitter period in which Croatian Serbs really did face genocide—the Second World War.

Tudjman talked of a 'Greater Croatia' and his party marched through Serbian populated towns under the slogan 'God in the Heavens and Tudjman in the Homelands'.[34] As one of Tudjman's former advisers admitted:

> We should have politically disarmed the Serbs in Croatia by promising them cultural autonomy and rights...we left it too late. Last year's election campaign by the Christian Democratic Union was won on a Croatian nationalist programme. Tudjman insisted that all Serbs take an oath of loyalty to the Croatian state. This played into the hands of Serbian nationalists and Slobodan Milosevic, who keeps accusing us of being fascist.

In August 1990 Serbs in Croatia voted for Serbian autonomy. The Croat authorities rejected the vote and ordered that arms of police reserve units in the Serb dominated areas be reduced by 60 percent, sparking off Serbian riots on 28 and 29 September in Petrinka, Dvor na Uni and Donji Lapac near Knin.[35]

Events in Serbia itself, however, showed how the long fermenting brew of economic discontent, disillusionment with the Communists and the activities of the nationalists were working to create a situation in which the party bosses could only hope to survive by drawing their strategy to its bloody conclusion—warfare. Early in 1991 thousands of Serbian workers protested outside the Republic Assembly building in Belgrade, demanding months of back pay which had been withheld. A general strike by metal and textile workers was narrowly averted after a similar incident. The *Financial Times* reported:

> The unchallenged power of Mr Slobodan Milosevic, the Socialist (former Communist) president, was put to the test after tens of thousands of people took to the streets to protest against the Socialist (former Communist) Party's grip over the media. Two people were killed, and 90 were wounded. Mr Milosevic panicked. He telephoned the army six times to quash the demonstrations to save him. The army eventually arrived but stayed only for a day. Mr Milosevic was not saved by the army. He was saved by his arch-rival, President Tudjman. On March 25 both

men met secretly in Karadjordjevo, in Serbia. There an agreement was apparently reached to overthrow Mr Markovic and carve up Bosnia-Hercegovina, which would be shared between Serbia and Croatia. Two days later 50,000 people demonstrated in Belgrade to press their demands for press freedom. April was just as tense. The federal government condemned moves by Slovenia and Croatia to secede; anti-army demonstrations were held in Croatia; 700,000 workers went on strike in Serbia; the presidents of the six republics agreed to hold a referendum on the future of the country by June 1991. In May, the rhetoric of hatred and violence between Serbs and Croats spilled onto the streets.[36]

On 25 June both Croatia and Slovenia declared their independence. Immediately afterwards, the federal army moved into Slovenia, ostensibly to secure the external border, in reality to subjugate the territory. They could not have bargained on the resistance they met. Tanks rumbled into the streets of Ljubljana, but the Slovenes were no pushover. The local authorities had substantial supplies of arms and the battle quickly spread across the republic. Every adult Yugoslav knows the tactics for absorbing and holding down a superior invading force. The military strategy of Yugoslavia was designed around this principle to make either a NATO or Warsaw Pact invasion too risky to contemplate. Now the Slovenes turned it against an unforeseen enemy. Helicopters were shot down, tanks disabled and soon the until then multinational army lost its resolve to fight.

Now, however, the conflict had moved on to a much more dangerous field, Croatia. Here the battle has been of a different nature altogether. The army has now become effectively a tool of Serbia. The heady mix of nationalism generated over the previous two years was enough to ensure that the regular army would be supported by a bitter and armed Serb population. Here there was no question of Serbs losing the will to fight as quickly as in Slovenia. In many cases the irregular soldiers, charged with nationalism and bigotry as they were, were actually fighting for their own houses and villages. By the middle of September it was clear that, regardless of what schemes either Milosevic or Tudjman might have had for dividing up the country, they were now locked into a vicious cycle from which there was no easy escape.

The offensive against Slovenia had already cracked the army as a federal institution. Now federal control was lost completely after the presidency tried to order it out of Croatia. It stayed, because an ending of the war would mean a return to all the old problems. The nationalist banner would be seized by those such as Vuk Draskovic of the Serbian

Renewal Party. Economic discontent would well to the surface again. The logic of the situation has also drawn the army into Bosnia and could take them to Macedonia. In either instance the war will widen and grow more complex. Pogroms will spread. Retreat will become yet more difficult.

With such an apparently desperate situation, many have been tempted to call for a solution from outside. But no Western power is going to defend the Albanians, or be interested in smoothing over the antagonisms between Serbs and Croats which they spent half a century promoting. Their economic 'remedies' have already been tried over the last 25 years. Anyway, the Western powers are split. Britain has the experience of Northern Ireland to worry about. While Tudjman based his strategy on the prospect of assistance from the German government, such support has been muted. The French government complicated matters even more by secretly favouring a victory for Serbia.

If large numbers of troops do get sent in to pull the northern republics away from Serbia and into the EC fold, then they could get bogged down for years. The fighting in Croatia has been bloody because it is a struggle over partition. The precedents for outsiders involving themselves in such battles are still present to be seen in Belfast and Cyprus. The events have shown that the rulers of Yugoslavia can only divide with their nationalism. Milosevic, Tudjman and Kucan have nothing to offer except pogroms and communalism.

Are there voices opposing this madness? By the end of September only small signs of resistance to the slide into nationalist mayhem had arisen. Polls have consistently found that 20 percent of all Yugoslavs consider themselves anti-nationalist.[37] More concretely, movements have grown in both Zagreb and Belgrade among the mothers of those sent to the front. Initially at least, the ideas driving these movements were extremely confused. A demonstrating mother in Belgrade demanded the return of her son from Slovenia, but then said, 'If they do not come home, I want Slovene boys to be taken hostage'.[38] Such, however, were the first stirrings of opposition to the Vietnam War. More significantly, there was a revolt of soldiers in Velika Plana in Serbia itself in mid-September.[39] These are straws in the wind certainly, but crucial signs that the cycle of workers' revolt, followed by increased nationalism which in turn fails to satisfy workers' real needs, is far from finished.

When socialists talk about there being an alternative between socialism and barbarism, it has a real meaning in Yugoslavia. Here we have seen a battle between classes in which the ruling class has only been able to forestall defeat by deflecting it towards nationalism, and then war. The strikes which even in April 1991 threatened to topple Milosevic may once again resume and lay the basis for new battles in which there will be a potential for working class unity. Trotsky wrote at the time of the Balkan Wars that the whole history of the region compels a choice between two alternatives—workers' unity from below, or war and misery imposed from above:

> Unity of the Balkan peninsula can be achieved in two ways: either from above, by expanding one Balkan state, whichever proves strongest, at the expense of the weaker ones—this is the road of wars of extermination and oppression of weak nations, a road that consolidates monarchism and militarism; or from below, through the peoples themselves coming together—this is the road of revolution, the road that means overthrowing the Balkan dynasties and unfurling the banner of a Balkan federal republic.[40]

This will not be achieved today by abstract appeals to the brotherhood of nations. Serbian workers will have to confront arguments from other Serbian workers that nothing can be achieved by backing the forced unity of Yugoslavia through war—that road only leads back to supporting their own economic tormentor, Slobodan Milosevic. Croatian workers will have to come up against arguments that, while they want the army out of Croatia, the biggest obstacle to achieving this is Franjo Tudjman, whose nationalism constantly drives on the Serbs of Croatia against the Croats. Everywhere the argument will have to be that here is a mess created by the system to which all the contending leaders subscribe. Genuine socialists in Yugoslavia will have to do as the Bolsheviks did in the Tsarist empire—stand against all attempts to push nations around, but insist that only an independent workers' movement is capable of such a solution. The other alternative is barbarism, which almost certainly won't mean Tudjman, or Milosevic, or the Western powers benefiting from the situation. It could well mean a meltdown in which every side loses—the common ruin of all contending classes.

Notes

1   *Newsweek*, 8 July 1991.
2   *Financial Times*, 27 May 1991.
3   *Guardian*, 21 September 1991.
4   H Poulton, *The Balkans, Minorities and States in Conflict* (London, 1990), p1.
5   Ibid, p2.
6   Ibid, p35.
7   Ibid, p7.
8   I Barac, *The National Question in Yugoslavia* (Cornell, 1984), p131.
9   Ibid, p 138.
10 R Pearson, *National Minorities in Eastern Europe 1848-1945* (London, 1983).
11 *Yugoslavery* (London, 1991), p9.
12 The assertion that Serbo-Croat is one rather than two languages seems to cause some consternation. Admittedly, there are differences between the Serbian and Croatian versions, but these are no more marked than the differences of dialect within the two versions. The principal difference is between the two alphabets, Latin and Cyrillic, in Croatia and Serbia respectively. But Turkish did not become a new language when it was officially converted to the Latin script in 1908. Misha Glenny records 'Srbija je ustala' (Serbia has arisen) and 'Hrvatska je ustala' (Croatia has arisen) as the mutually understandable, mutually hostile cries of 1989. M Glenny, *The Rebirth of History: Eastern Europe in the Age of Democracy* (London, 1990), p142.
13 L J Cohen, *The Socialist Pyramid: Elites in Power in Yugoslavia* (London, 1989), pp303-308.
14 B MacFarlane, *Yugoslavia: Politics, Economy and Society* (London, 1988), p78.
15 See for instance, R Bolland, 'Croatian Nationalism', *Socialist Review* (Melbourne, 1990).
16 *New Left Review* 174, p20.
17 H Poulton, op cit, p59.
18 *Problems of Communism*, March-April 1983 (Washington), pp65-70.
19 Ibid, p65.
20 *BBC Survey of World Broadcasts* EE/0305, 10 November 1988.
21 *Problems of Communism*, op cit, p61.
22 *New Left Review* 174, p21.
23 M Glenny, op cit, p122.
24 *New Left Review* 174, p31.
25 *Financial Times*, 27 June 1991.
26 Ibid.
27 *New Left Review* 174, p5.
28 M Glenny, op cit, pp125-126.
29 Ibid, pp125-126.
30 H Poulton, op cit, p37.
31 *Financial Times*, 27 June 1991.
32 M Glenny, op cit, p 128.
33 *Financial Times*, 27 June 1991.
34 H Poulton, op cit, p33.
35 Ibid, p26.

36   *Financial Times*, 27 June 1991.
37   *Guardian*, 24 June 1991.
38   *Financial Times*, 4 July 1991.
39   *Financial Times*, 21 September 1991.
40   L Trotsky, 'The Balkan Question and Social Democracy', in L Trotsky, *The Balkan Wars* (New York, 1980), p40.

Chapter 8

Balkan tragedy

Chris Bambery

Is this really part of Europe? That must be the question many people are asking as they view the bloody civil war which is raging in what was Yugoslavia.

As ceasefire after ceasefire breaks down, it is very tempting to see the divisions within the Balkans as being intractable, somehow built into the region and its people.

Yet this is not the case. The borders of this region were deliberately created in order to foster divisions and prevent the emergence of a strong, unified nation. The great powers of Europe plotted this process, using various countries in the area as proxies in their rivalries. This strategy led at the beginning of this century to two bloody wars and would in turn produce the spark for the horrors of the First World War.

Leon Trotsky, exiled to Vienna after the failed Russian Revolution of 1905, went as a war correspondent for the radical Ukrainian paper *Kievan Thought* to cover both Balkan Wars which took place in 1912 and 1913. His writings are a triumph of journalism, catching the horrors of both wars and exposing official censorship which covered up the massacres of prisoners and civilians. They also provide an explanation of the causes of these bloody conflicts which is equally relevant today.

The vast bulk of the Balkans had fallen under Turkish control in the Middle Ages. The Ottoman Empire was able to advance from its centre in Asia Minor into a power vacuum. The Byzantine Empire—the remains of the former Roman Empire based in Constantinople (now Istanbul)—was reduced to little more than the city itself and some territory in Greece.

Across the region the vast majority of the peasantry remained neutral between their old rulers and the Ottomans. Many welcomed the

First published November 1991

new order and converted to Islam. In 1389 the Serbian king was killed and his nobility destroyed at the Battle of Kosovo. Three years later much of what is now Romania was under Ottoman rule. Five years after that the medieval kingdom of Bulgaria was destroyed, and by the middle of the next century Constantinople had fallen and Greece was under Turkish control.

At its high water mark Turkish expansion twice reached the gates of Vienna. But after the failure of the second siege in 1683, the Ottoman Empire was pushed increasingly back. By the 19th century the various European powers were casting their eyes over Turkish possessions in the Balkans.

The Austro-Hungarian Empire was a ramshackle affair. Centred on its traditional base in German speaking Austria, the bulk of its territory was populated by Hungarians, Czechs, Slovaks, Poles and Romanians, with significant German and Jewish communities mixed in. Blocked by Tsarist Russia to the east and to the west by Prussia and the eventual unification of Germany, the Austro-Hungarian Empire in Vienna could only expand southwards into what is now Serbia. Croatia was in the front line between the Austro-Hungarian and Ottoman empires for centuries. In order both to control Croatia and to defend the border regions, Vienna encouraged Serbs fleeing from Ottoman rule to settle along Croatia's borders.

Tsarist Russia hoped it could wield dominant influence over its fellow Slavs in the region. It faced rivalry in the Balkans not just from the Austro-Hungarian Empire. For much of the 19th century it was at daggers drawn with Britain, which wanted control of the Mediterranean. In the 1820s British intervention secured independence from Ottoman rule for Greece.

In the face of the expansion of Russian influence in the region, Britain determined to prop up the decaying Ottoman Empire. Throughout the 19th century there were a series of conflicts.

In 1853 this entailed full scale war in the Crimea between Russia on the one side and Britain, France and Turkey on the other. In 1876 Serbia and Montenegro went to war with the Ottomans. This sparked a national revolt in Bulgaria. Seizing the chance Russia and Romania joined in, as did Greece.

The resulting peace treaty was so favourable to Russia that Britain, Germany and Austria imposed a new treaty on Moscow which outlined the borders of the various new states and granted the three European powers various 'spheres of influence' over Ottoman possessions.

Trotsky summed up the results of all this:

The states that today occupy the Balkan peninsula were manufactured by European diplomacy around the table at the Congress of Berlin in 1878. There it was that all the measures were taken to convert the national diversity of the Balkans into a regular *mêlée* of petty states. None of them was to develop beyond a certain limit, each separately was entangled in diplomatic and dynastic bonds and counterposed to all the rest, and finally the whole lot were condemned to helplessness in relation to the Great Powers of Europe and their continual intrigues and machinations. Part of the territory inhabited by the Bulgars was detached from Turkey by the congress and transformed into a vassal principality.

It was the intervention of the Great Powers (now including the unified states of Germany and Italy) which prevented the unification of the Slavic peoples of the Balkans into a national state, and—on the basis of that—any significant industrialisation.

The various states which were thrown up swung in allegiance between the Great Powers. Over each stood a monarch often chosen by the powers. None experienced democracy and all were trapped in a pattern of economic underdevelopment. As Trotsky wrote:

The Balkan peninsula, which is approximately as big as Germany but has only about one third as many inhabitants (22 million), is divided between six independent states: Greece, Turkey, Romania, Bulgaria, Serbia and Montenegro, together with the Austro-Hungarian provinces of Dalmatia, Bosnia and Hercegovina. In the six independent states, each of which has its own dynasty, army, currency and customs system, there live many nations and races, divided into separate fragments: Greeks, Turks, Romanians, Bulgars, Serbs, Albanians, Jews, Armenians, Gypsies... The frontiers between the dwarf states of the Balkan peninsula were drawn not in accordance with national conditions or national demands, but as a result of wars, diplomatic intrigues and dynastic interests. The Great Powers—in the first place, Russia and Austria—have always had a direct interest in setting the Balkan peoples and states against each other and then, when they have weakened one another, subjecting them to their economic and political influence.

Of the problems facing the region Trotsky pinpointed the major one:

First and foremost stands the *national question*. The motley composition of the population of Turkey, as regards nationality and religion, results in powerful centrifugal tendencies. The old regime thought it could overcome these by mechanical weight of the army, recruited extensively from Muslims. In fact, however, this brought about the disintegration of the state. In Abdul Hamid's [theTurkish sultan from 1876 to 1909] reign alone Turkey lost Bulgaria, Eastern Rumelia, Bosnia and Hercegovina, Egypt, Tunisia and the Dobruja. Asia Minor has fallen helplessly under the economic and political dictatorship of Germany... No end could be seen to the dismemberment of Turkey. Yet an extensive and economically unified territory is a necessary precondition for industrial development. This applies not only to Turkey but to the Balkan peninsula as a whole. It is not its national diversity but the fact of its splintering into many states that weighs upon the latter like a curse. Customs frontiers divide it artificially into separate bits. The machinations of the capitalist powers are interwoven with the bloody intrigues of the Balkan dynasties. If these conditions continue, the Balkan peninsula will go on being a Pandora's Box.

Trotsky argued that capitalism was incapable of overcoming the problems of the region. The native ruling classes were too weak and servile. The European powers could meddle and divide but could not bring progress.

Instead Trotsky cut through all this in arguing, along with fellow socialists in the region, for a socialist federation of the Balkans with guarantees for all minorities.

At the beginning of this century the instability of the region was deepened as Great Power rivalries intensified. From 1871 onwards Germany exerted more and more influence on the region. The Austro-Hungarian Empire was increasingly dependent upon Berlin, and its influence grew over Constantinople. Britain and Germany were now pitted against each other as the main imperialist powers. Germany signed a treaty with Austria and Italy. Britain entered a pact with France and Russia. As part of this, Britain and Russia entered agreement on a division of the Ottoman Empire between them.

This agreement triggered a crisis in the Ottoman Empire. A section of the army, the civil service and business interests understood that the existing empire could not withstand pressure from London and Moscow. They wanted to create a modern state.

In July 1908 the Turkish army in Macedonia, under the control of officers belonging to the Young Turk movement, rose up, marched on Constantinople and forced the sultan to declare a constitution. Taking advantage of this, Austria formally seized Bosnia and Hercegovina whilst

Bulgaria declared its independence. When, the following year, the sultan tried to organise a counter-coup, the army toppled him.

The new military rulers of Turkey increased their links with Germany. The 'Great Game' of 19th century, diplomatic intrigue, was turning increasingly bloody.

In the autumn of 1912 Montenegro, Serbia, Bulgaria and Greece formed a Balkan League and agreed to seize Turkey's remaining Balkan territories and divide them between them. Each had their eyes on particular prizes. Serbia wanted access to the sea via Albania. Greece wanted Salonika and other areas to its north. Bulgaria wanted Macedonia. In October they launched their attack. Within a month the Turkish forces were driven back almost to Constantinople. Turkey sued for peace. The peace terms accepted by the sultan were so humiliating they provoked a coup by the Young Turks, who resumed the war. But with no chance of success, they were forced to return to the peace table.

The Great Powers now became alarmed at events. Austria did not wish Serbia to have access to the Adriatic. When Serbian troops took the Albanian port of Durrës, Austria threatened to intervene. Serbia appealed to its protector, Russia, for help, but the Tsar would not intervene. The resulting peace treaty was imposed by the Great Powers. Albania was declared independent. Bulgaria, which had borne the costs of the war, was denied territory in Macedonia, which was divided between Greece and Serbia.

In June 1913, Bulgaria launched a lightning attack on Greek and Serbian positions in Macedonia. Seizing the chance, Romania and Turkey attacked Bulgaria. Bulgaria was forced to accept a treaty which granted Romania a tranche of its northern territory, expanded Turkey's remaining toe hold in Europe and confirmed Greek and Serbian hold on the bulk of Macedonia.

Trotsky summed up the results of these two wars thus:

> It must be said, therefore, about the new boundary lines in the Balkan peninsula, regardless of how long they may last, that they have been drawn across the living bodies of nations that have been lacerated, bled white and exhausted. Not one of these Balkan nations has succeeded in gathering together all its scattered fragments. And, at the same time, every one of the Balkan states, including Romania, now includes within its borders a compact minority that is hostile to it.
>
> Such are the fruits of war that swallowed up—in killed, wounded and dead from disease—not less than half a million men. Not a single one of the basic problems of Balkan development has been solved.

Today the Balkan question has emerged centre stage again. Trotsky's warning of 1913 rings clear:

The Eastern Question burns still, discharging poison like a frightful ulcer, in the body of capitalist Europe.

Chapter 9

Intervention: disease or cure?

Alex Callinicos

The Western establishment continues to be deeply divided over the issue of military intervention in the Balkan war. While the Clinton administration has been pressing its European allies to take part in armed action against the Bosnian Serbs, it has faced considerable opposition at home. In Britain, while one Tory ex prime minister, Lady Thatcher, has called for Western intervention on the side of the Bosnian government, another, Edward Heath, has vigorously opposed the idea.

While many on the right are dubious about the merits of intervention, much of the left is stridently in favour of it. Staunch opponents of the Gulf War now demand that the troops who devastated Iraq be used to bring peace to the Balkans. Three of the firmest opponents of US foreign policy in the Reagan-Bush era—Noam Chomsky, Christopher Hitchens and Edward Said—have effectively sided with Thatcher, that policy's strongest European defender, in denouncing the West's 'pseudo-evenhandedness that has, in fact, strengthened the side of aggressive Serb expansionism', and calling for the United Nations arms embargo on Bosnia to be scrapped.

The *New Statesman*, which published this appeal, did acknowledge that 'the left is as divided as the international community over what should be done in Bosnia', and then proceeded to offer three 'different views', all of which happened to agree on the need for intervention! One of these, by Ken Cole, an ex-member of CND and the Peace Pledge Union, was particularly revealing of the prevalent confusion: 'I tend towards pacifist views—but that doesn't mean that I am opposed to any kind of military action.'

First published June 1993

The same pattern—of pacifists in favour of war, anti-imperialists calling for the US Marines to go in—was evident in the House of Commons debate on Bosnia at the end of April. While John Smith [the Labour leader] called for limited air strikes against the Serbs, several left wing Labour backbenchers went much further. Chris Mullin, former editor of *Tribune*, declared, 'It is, unhappily, a fact of life that only a credible force, military force on the ground, not bombing, is going to make any difference.' Ken Livingstone, one of the most prominent opponents of the Gulf War, demanded that troops be sent in, 'as many as it takes for as long as it takes'.

Of course the basis on which right wingers oppose and left wingers support intervention is different. Right wing objections tend to be pragmatic, focusing on the difficulties of mounting large scale military operations in the former Yugoslavia. They were admirably summarised by the Tory military historian Correlli Barnett:

> It is perfectly plain…that Bosnia as a state within its old frontiers is a lost cause, short of the deployment of Western armed forces on the scale of Desert Storm, at the least. Such an offensive campaign would not be like Desert Storm, a technologically updated Battle of Omdurman, but instead a long, slogging struggle with colossal logistical commitments and heavy casualties.

Left wing pro-interventionists are much more disposed to appeal to high principle. They denounce 'aggressive Serb expansionism'. They are fond of comparing, as Livingstone did, Serb 'aggrandisement' to Hitler's in the 1930s. And they frequently liken opponents of intervention to the Western governments which appeased the Nazis at Munich in 1938.

It's surprising that the pro-interventionists never pause to examine these arguments' credentials. The example of Munich and the 'lesson' that aggression can only be halted by force has been used to justify, among other things, the Anglo-French attempt to seize the Suez Canal in 1956, the deployment of Cruise missiles in Europe in the early 1980s, Britain's use of force to recapture the Falklands in 1982, and, most recently, the US led coalition's war against its former ally Saddam Hussein.

The pro-intervention arguments proceed from a false premise— that the war is a consequence of Serb aggression. It is, in fact, a war of partition being waged chiefly by the two main successor states of the old Yugoslav federal republic, Serbia under Slobodan Milosevic and

Croatia under Franjo Tudjman, each pursuing expansionist policies.

The origins of both the Milosevic and Tudjman regimes lie in the profound socio-economic crisis which gripped the old order in Yugoslavia in the 1980s. As in the other state capitalist countries in Eastern Europe, the bureaucratic command economy went into terminal decline, exacerbated in Yugoslavia by its much greater degree of integration into the world market than other Stalinist states. A huge foreign debt, galloping inflation, mass unemployment—all these factors helped produce intense class polarisation which reached its climax in a wave of mass strikes in 1987-88.

Under the pressure of this crisis, the ruling class of bureaucrats and managers began to fragment. The slump had in any case widened the fault lines between the different republics—in particular between the relatively prosperous northern republics of Slovenia and Croatia, and the poorer south dominated by Serbia. Some Stalinist politicians began to see that by seizing on particular nationalisms they could rebuild the mass base they had lost.

Milosevic was the first to do this, beating the drum of Serb nationalism and seizing control of the predominantly Albanian province of Kosovo. But he soon found ready imitators in the 'liberal' bureaucrats of Slovenia, and Tudjman, who took power in Croatia in the spring of 1990. The clash of these rival nationalisms engulfed the Balkans in war.

The Tudjman regime has come under much less critical scrutiny than its Serb counterpart, reflecting its powerful Western supporters, most notably the entire German political establishment. It has also found apologists on the left—for example, Branka Magas and Quintin Hoare. This is surprising since Tudjman is a Holocaust revisionist, the author of a book which claimed that the wartime pro-Nazi Ustashe state in Croatia hadn't killed large numbers of Jews, Serbs, and Muslims. Tudjman's presence at the recent opening of the Holocaust Museum in Washington caused outrage among prominent Jewish figures.

On taking office Tudjman adopted the Ustashe flag, purged Serbs from public sector jobs and replaced Serb with Croat policeman in the predominantly Serb parts of Croatia such as the Krajina, helping to drive the Serb minority in Croatia into Milosevic's arms, and making it easier for the Yugoslav National Army (JNA) and its Serb allies to seize 30 percent of Croatian territory in the second half of 1991. Meanwhile, as early as March 1991, Milosevic and Tudjman met to discuss dividing Bosnia-Hercegovina between them.

The Milosevic and Tudjman regimes are mirrors of one another. As Mary Kaldor puts it:

> Both leaders are creatures of the old totalitarian structures... Both use the ideology of nationalism to generate the same sort of war psychosis that was typically used by Stalinists. The Croatian government has actually renationalised property and now controls 90 percent of the economy, with former members of the *nomenklatura* in key positions. Both leaders tightly control the electronic media and both leaders eavesdrop on members of the opposition. If anything, the media is more tightly controlled in Croatia than in Serbia. There is, of course, one very important difference, and that is the fact that Serbians control the remnants of the JNA and its weaponry, though it is not quite clear who is in charge. But this is a difference not in the political nature of the two nationalisms but in the scale of power.

But is the Muslim led government of Bosnia-Hercegovina different? Chomsky and his co-authors, for example, praise 'its commitment to a democratic, multi-ethnic society'. There is some truth to this argument. Bosnia-Hercegovina is ethnically mixed (40 percent Muslim, 30 percent Serb, 17 percent Croat), and these labels fail to capture the reality of people who look and dress the same, speak the same language, and, especially in cities such as Sarajevo, have lived and worked together and intermarried. The government of Alia Izetbegovic has been based on a multi-ethnic coalition of parties wishing to preserve the old Bosnian republic.

The Bosnian regime nevertheless aligned itself in the larger war in former Yugoslavia, signing a formal alliance with Croatia, which effectively delivered large parts of Bosnia into Croatian hands. The HVO, the Croatian forces in Bosnia, have carved out their own state, Herceg-Bosnia, centred on Western Hercegovina. Cities such as Mostar, which successfully resisted a Serbian siege last year, are now under effective Croatian control. Ethnic cleansing by the HVO sparked off a wave of fighting between Croats and Muslims in Mostar at the beginning of May.

The extent of the Croatian betrayal of their Muslim allies can be best seen in central Bosnia. There, full scale fighting has developed between the HVO and the Muslim forces. Muslim military successes led the HVO to launch a wave of ethnic cleansing in the Muslim villages around Vitez. The resulting massacre of Muslim civilians in one of these villages reached the world's television screens. But it did not appear to lead any pro-interventionists to pause for thought and wonder if the Serbs really were the sole villains of the piece.

The Muslim forces have also adapted to the logic of ethno-territorial expansion unleashed by the Serbian and Croatian regimes. In the killing fields of central and eastern Bosnia all three antagonists practise ethnic cleansing—the Muslims of Srebrenica, for example, among Serb villages along the river Drina. The Serbian bombardment of Srebrenica on Easter Monday has been matched by the Croatian bombardment of Doboj—but only the first attracted the attention of the Western media.

Some argue that the relative weakness of the Bosnian government justifies intervention on its side. On the face of it, this is absurd. Why help the weakest side? Out of a sense of fair play? Moreover, this argument ignores the extent to which some of the actors in the war have built into their strategy appeals for outside support.

There is no reason to believe that the selective relaxation of the UN arms embargo in favour of the Bosnian Muslims would bring peace a step closer. The *Independent* recently quoted a British officer based in Vitez, who 'said it was a big mistake to think that Bosnian Muslims would attack the Serbs first if the arms embargo was lifted. "They are most likely to go for the weakest target, the Croat towns in central Bosnia," he said.' Arming the Muslims may thus simply intensify the three cornered savagery.

The other form of intervention favoured by Western leaders wary of deploying large ground forces in Bosnia is the use of air power. John Smith, Paddy Ashdown and David Owen have all advocated 'surgical' air strikes against Serb positions. But, as a stream of Pentagon generals were quick to point out, the risk of bombing causing large scale 'collateral damage'—civilian deaths—is high. 'Precision bombing' is a myth. The danger of civilian deaths would be especially high in Bosnia, where the war has caused large scale population movements which have dramatically swelled the size of villages like Srebrenica and cities like Tuzla. Since any military intervention would involve air strikes, Ken Livingstone and those who think like him should tell us how much collateral damage they are willing to accept.

The chief objection to intervention is, however, more fundamental. Intervention would be by the United States and the other Western great powers. Calls for a UN protectorate in Bosnia-Hercegovina simply obscure the real issue: the UN Security Council has become, since the end of the Cold War, a rubber stamp for US foreign policy.

The US, France and Britain call the shots. The other two permanent members, Russia and China, have to be kept on board, but both are heavily dependent on Western economic cooperation.

For centuries the Balkans have been an arena for Great Power rivalries—the Habsburg monarchy versus the Ottoman Empire between the 16th and 18th centuries; in the early 20th century, as Turkish power declined, Austria-Hungary backed by Germany versus Russia backed by France and Britain; during the Second World War the Axis powers versus the Allies.

Yugoslavia was created under Serbian hegemony after the First World War by French and British imperialism. It was pulled apart in 1941 by the German occupying army, which set up the Ustashe regime in Croatia. Restored after the war thanks chiefly to the Stalinist led multi-ethnic partisan movement, Yugoslavia survived through the Cold War because its existence suited the interests of both Eastern and Western blocs.

It is no coincidence that Yugoslavia fell apart in the wake of the 1989 revolutions which ended the superpower partition of Europe. Reunified Germany was able to sabotage the initial US policy of trying to hold Yugoslavia together, and secure EC recognition of Croatia and Slovenia. The terms of Bosnian independence were also laid down by the EC. By providing for the division of the republic into three ethnic 'cantons', the EC brokered agreement gave an open invitation to ethnic cleansing. The Vance-Owen plan takes the process of partition further, dividing Bosnia into ten ethnic provinces.

Undoubtedly one motive that is at work in the minds of the pro-intervention lobby in Washington is to show Germany and the rest of the EC that European security still depends on US military and political leadership. The Balkans are still an arena for Great Power rivalries. To imagine they can change their spots is naive.

The Bosnian war is merely one of a number of wars currently going on around the world. The war in Angola, and that between the ex-Soviet republics of Armenia and Azerbaijan are at least as bloody and destructive as the fighting in Bosnia. Former Yugoslavia has received the attention of Western governments and media because of its strategic location at the edge of one of the three main zones of advanced capitalism, the EC. But the Balkan war, like its counterparts in the former Soviet Union, and in the Third World, highlights the fact that the fall of Stalinism has ushered in, not George Bush's New World Order, or Francis Fukuyama's 'end of history', but a more dangerous and violent world.

Much of the Western left recognise this, but, out of despair and because many have been disorientated by the collapse of what they believed was 'existing socialism', look to the main centre of power in the world—Western imperialism—to prevent total anarchy. But this is to confuse the disease with its cure. The reason why the centre cannot hold isn't a lack of will or the wrong policy but because the Great Powers are part of, and chief beneficiaries from, a social and economic system that is based on anarchy and competition and which gives rise to crises, wars and revolutions. The only sure way to stop the killing in Bosnia and elsewhere is to get rid of this system.

We should remember that lying behind the slaughter that has gripped the Balkans in the past two years is a vast but displaced social conflict—the collapse of the old order in Yugoslavia during the 1980s. As the war grinds on, the terrible price it is exacting from working people, especially in Serbia and Croatia in the shape of unemployment and reduced living standards, is likely to reawaken that conflict. The privations of war may lead workers to discover that their real enemies are the regimes which set them at war with one another. A dream, you may say. But remember the First World War, which began with the workers of Europe marching under national flags to slaughter each other, and ended up with those same workers rising up against their rulers. That means turning towards class struggle as the only real basis for ending the war.

Chapter 10

Bosnia: the war within a war

Andreja Zivkovic

The Western media has bought the biggest lie peddled by the nationalist demagogues who have plunged ex-Yugoslavia into civil war. The picture is of a violent, irrational Balkan mentality that arises from deep within the history of the peoples of the region, periodically sending them into vicious cycles of bloodletting. We only see victims, the Bosnian Muslims, and criminals, Serbs and Croats, whose conflicts can only be solved from the outside.

But there is another story, of the 'war' within the war. It is the story of the Serbian and Croatian leaderships' attempts to maintain internal 'unity', and of workers' and ethnic minorities' protests against the war. It is a story untold by the newspapers or television reports.

The various ethnic leaderships have attempted to maintain power by setting the workers of the region at each other's throats. Yet nationalism has never been totally dominant among the mass of workers, who have combined a degree of support for national chauvinism with the pursuit of basic class aims. Thus workers in Croatia, while supporting a strong hand against the Serbian separatists in Krajina, do not support the war of partition being waged in Bosnia, and also reject Tudjman's right wing authoritarian government.

In Serbia the strike of 70,000 metal and textile workers and the mass demonstrations against Milosevic of March 1991 forced him to bring his strategy to its bloody military conclusion. Similarly in September 1991, a few months before the war in Bosnia, economic struggles in the republic reached mass proportions, and in November 20,000 Muslims, Croats and Serbs went on strike in Sarajevo to demand back wages owed.

First published September 1993

The unpopularity of the civil war means that opposition exists, although its form has been sporadic, isolated, passive and pacifist. Nevertheless it has been a constant thorn in the side of the Croatian and Serbian regimes. A mass demonstration of 100,000 workers, led by soldiers' mothers, took place in Sarajevo in July 1991 in the 'insurrection for peace'. In June 1992 a student strike and sit down protest in Belgrade against the war involved 20,000 and sparked a sympathy strike of higher education workers.

The demonstrations in Serbia over the last year have mainly been confined to students and white collar workers, and have been influenced by the nationalist politics of the democratic opposition. During the period of pacifist opposition, which looks as if it is beginning to crack open, most opposition by the broad masses to the war took the form of draft dodging and desertion.

Milosevic and Tudjman have consistently conspired to prevent, isolate and repress any resistance to their power. In Croatia the former state unions offered the government a no-strike deal for the duration of the war, whilst their counterparts in Serbia provided a transmission belt for Milosevic's Greater Serbian nationalism. It was only in May this year that a one hour general strike was called in Croatia to recognise the independent trade unions, which was supported by over half of the workforce, forcing Tudjman to ask his cabinet to resign.

Both Tudjman and Milosevic have also attempted to control their respective media to prevent alternative voices being heard. An independent press barely exists in Croatia—recently the last anti-government daily, *Slobodna Dalmacija*, was put under direct HDZ control, although not before a strike by the journalists had been defeated. In Serbia, Milosevic's control over state television allows him to exploit the fact that 90 percent of the population depend on television for the majority of their news information, as hyper-inflation has made newspapers a luxury for ordinary people. Milosevic has purged thousands of 'ideologically unsound' employees in radio, television and the public sector. Tudjman has put critical journalists on trial for 'treason against the Croatian state'.

The nationalism of the organised 'democratic' opposition to the regimes has legitimised the national carnage and ensured that Milosevic and Tudjman have remained in power. Disagreements are usually about how to achieve 'Greater Serbia' or 'Historic Croatia'. Peace activists and intellectuals have so far failed to link up social discontent with opposition to the war. Their representatives often see workers as in some way responsible for the policies of their rulers. However, some peace activists are beginning to take a much more militant stand.

While accepting on a certain level Milosevic's argument that the Serbian nation was in danger from all sides, workers and youth have consistently refused to die for a Greater Serbia. The deep unpopularity of the war is reflected in the percentage of reservists who have avoided conscription—in Belgrade 85 percent and in Serbia proper 50 percent—and in the fact that 200,000 young men have left the country. Opposition to conscription is sharpened by the question of class. Raw conscripts have been sent to the front while incompetent generals have sat in the rear. The government has in effect ceased prosecution of draft dodgers since the courts are simply unable to deal with the workload, with 10,000 cases pending.

In the autumn of 1991 some 200 reservists in Kosieric, eastern Serbia, protested that only the sons of workers and peasants were being sent to the front. They deposed the town council, elected their own reserve officer as mayor and demanded the resignation of the defence minister. They held the town for two days before conceding to the threats of army intervention. Protests against conscription also took place in Belgrade, Kraljevo, Bogatic and Kragujevac.

In November 1991 a wider revolt broke out in Vojvodina, where Milosevic was attempting to use ethnic Hungarians, and to a lesser extent Serbs, as cannon fodder. He feared that workers in Serbia itself would not tolerate bearing the whole brunt of mobilisation. The planned mobilisation of a Territorial Defence Unit in Senta—80 percent of whose population is ethnic Hungarian—provoked a spontaneous rebellion of reservists and townspeople. The people of Senta demanded an emergency session of the municipal assembly, which conducted a referendum asking the citizens whether they supported the war and whether they felt they should take part in it. Rebellion spread to Ada, where over 1,000 came to hear Hungarian and Serb anti-war activists, and to other towns. The authorities in Novi Sad branded the revolt a Hungarian plot acting as the 'fifth column of Croat fascist hordes' and met it with repression.

The war in Bosnia has effectively smothered any real multi-ethnic resistance. Tragically this is not only the work of the proxies of Zagreb and Belgrade. The Muslim leadership has been sucked into the logic of ethnic cleansing and has committed atrocities against the Serb villages around Srebrenica and against the Croats of central Bosnia. In fighting for a Muslim state it has employed Mujahadeen from Afghanistan and

Revolutionary Guards from Iran, who despise the multi-ethnic traditions of Bosnia, as its shock troops.

Those who confuse multi-ethnic resistance with the Bosnian Muslim militias are unable to explain why towns like Tuzla, Mostar and Zenica, that were until recently a model of inter-communal living, should have disintegrated so easily from within when threatened from without. In the face of a bitter three sided civil war where the practice of the Muslim militias has been to treat all Serbs and Croats as equally guilty, it is not surprising that suspicion can spread like the plague.

The actions of the Muslim militias in the struggle for central Bosnia has allowed Tudjman to make a smooth propaganda shift—from being loyal 'allies' against the Serbs, the Muslims have become 'Islamic fundamentalist hordes' threatening Christian civilisation. The questions many Croats might have asked themselves about the policies of their leaders have been silenced by the destruction of the Croatian villages around Travnik.

This should not surprise us. The Serbian-Croatian attempt to partition the republic forced the Muslim leadership to fight for its own national state. It demanded UN intervention against the Serbs, and then the Croats, and in the process alienated those it claims would have national rights in an independent Bosnia. It is thus a player in the game; a weak one, maybe, but nevertheless not part of any solution to the conflict. Arming the Muslims will not break the logic of ethnic cleansing, nor will it contribute to inter-ethnic unity.

Despite the pressure that has even forced mixed families to take sides there have been sporadic rejections of this barbaric logic. The Croatian and Muslim communities of Fojnica recently demanded that General Morillon of the UN declare the town a peace zone since they refused to fight in the war. The district president Mijat Tuka said, 'The danger is that the BIH [mainly Bosnian Muslim army] and the HVO [Bosnian Croat army] will have plans for Fojnica.' A week later the town was bombed by the Muslim militia. In the mixed town of Tesanj in central Bosnia the people refused to allow the HVO or the BIH to control their militia and declared that they would defend their town against all sides.

These gestures reflect the vague feeling amongst a significant minority of Bosnians—Croats, Muslims and to a lesser extent Serbs—that no side really represents their interests. This gut feeling leads them to continue to hope for reconciliation even after all the suffering that they have endured. Yet its organised expression has been crushed by all sides.

The apparent endgame that is being played out on the merry go round of the Geneva peace talks is unlikely to be resolved in the near future. Air strikes against the Serbs are not a solution to the conflict since they do not question the partition of Bosnia on ethnic lines. It is not even clear that the European powers are prepared to allow themselves to be sucked into what they see as the wolf's lair by the US.

The Great Powers are only concerned to maintain regional stability. The problem they face is that Sarajevo has become such a potent symbol of what the Vance-Owen Plan helped to destroy that to openly support a Serbian-Croatian carve up of Bosnia is almost impossible. In the short term their empty sabre rattling will merely increase nationalism amongst ordinary Serbs. Thousands have already demonstrated against UN intervention in Banja Luka, Zvornik, Bijeljina and Trebinje. In any case, the key to the future of Bosnia lies in the balance of class forces in Belgrade and Zagreb.

The effect of the civil war and the economic blockade by the West on an already stagnant Serbian economy has been devastating. Most of industry is at a standstill and more than half the workforce is on obligatory leave because of the shortage of raw materials, semi-manufactures, fuel and other basic inputs. Hyper-inflation has reached an annual rate of a billion percent. Inflation is approaching 1 percent an hour. The average monthly salary is the equivalent of £2 whilst the average monthly cost of living is £12. Basic goods have disappeared from the shelves. Daily survival is predominant in most people's minds. Old people suffer most—their fixed monthly pensions have been rendered worthless. Aleksandar Vasovic writes of pensioners digging around in rubbish bins for food. In July pensioners sent a letter to Milosevic begging him to find a way to put them to sleep because they were starving and without hope.

Workers have taken matters into their own hands and gone out on strike without the permission of the official trade unions. In July 18,000 miners in the Kolubara region in Serbia came out on strike demanding payment of wages owed, as did the engineers of the Kusic metal works in Valjevo, while 10,000 workers in Viskoza chemical plant in Loznica threatened to blockade the city for the same reason. Workers at the massive Zastava car plant in Kragujevac planned to join the strikes. The government was forced to concede to their demands, a decision no doubt helped by the fact that the plant also houses the largest arms production site in ex-Yugoslavia.

Train drivers in Montenegro went out on strike for three days. Their colleagues in Serbia immediately voted to join them but called off their action when the government swiftly conceded to their demands. Air controllers at JAT have been on strike since mid-June despite victimisation. At the end of the month farmers in Vojvodina blockaded the republic's only road and rail links to the west for two days in protest against the effects of hyper-inflation on the already low price of grain. Despite police clearing them away with batons they have vowed to continue their resistance.

In August strikes broke out in oil producing plants and among slaughterhouse workers. Strikes began to take place on a daily basis. Aleksander Vasovic claims that 'around 10 percent of Serbian industry is on strike at any one time', and adds that while economic issues provide an immediate stimulus this is often accompanied by a 'constant anti-war feeling'. A general strike was called for 5 August by the (state) union confederation to prevent workers from 'going with the current and resolving vital problems of subsistence on the streets'. The union's president admitted that this was the last opportunity to funnel social unrest into ways that can still be controlled.

In the event—despite a million workers joining the strike—it was relatively unsuccessful. Essential services were maintained and many workers continued working. This was because the unions made a deal with the government on the eve of the strike, whereby the government accepted the majority of the strikers' demands, and the unions declared that they would review the situation on 1 September.

Hyper-inflation helps sharpen the class contradictions in Serbian society to an unbearable level. A decisive turning point is approaching. Workers are particularly sensitive to these counter-currents. On one level they continue to blame the West for the economic chaos, a feeling that threats of military intervention only serve to heighten. But on another level they feel that they must act in order to survive. This is combined with a hatred of the speculators who have made unimaginable fortunes from the war and who at the time of writing are to be found on the beaches of Hawaii and South America.

Milosevic is beginning to lose his halo of authority as workers ask awkward questions about the cost of the war—admittedly within nationalist terms of reference. Within the ruling class confusion abounds. Milosevic, criminal number one, has been forced to initiate a campaign against speculators and governmental corruption. In conceding to the economic demands of the strikers he has incurred the wrath of his former puppet Zoran Lific, the federal president, who is desperately trying to control inflation. Certain elements of the ruling class are beginning to despair at an economic policy that consists of endlessly printing money and periodically trying to rein in the price of certain basic goods.

This last factor is critical. Milosevic's politics are a combination of virulent populist nationalism and an ability to compromise. Sectors of the ruling class are no longer so ready to compromise. They are beginning to look to someone who will provide decisive leadership and 'national unity'. Vojislav Seselj, leader of the fascist Serbian Radical Party, is now a serious contender for power. He has significant support amongst the generals, the security services, the army rank and file, and the Serbs of Croatia, Bosnia and Vojvodina. A bloody coup beckons.

Milosevic can only reply by raising the nationalist stakes. That means a fight to the death against the increasingly organised and militant Albanian majority of Kosovo and in all probability a Balkan civil war as Macedonia is sucked into the nationalist whirlpool.

In these circumstances Serbian workers will have to confront nationalism in order to ward off the counter-revolution. Economic strikes are not enough. Only a political response to the crisis, with an understanding that their poverty is based on the oppression of other nationalities, can topple Milosevic and provide a lead to the other workers of the region. In doing so it can pull the rug from under the Serbian warlords of Bosnia and Croatia who preside over devastated economies.

Further, the struggle against Milosevic would provide food for thought for Croatian workers, whose frustration with the HDZ's corruption and economic incompetence is only curbed by the Serbian occupation of the east of the country.

Any calls for UN intervention in the region will only serve to shore up Serbian and Croatian domination in ex-Yugoslavia and will foster nationalist feelings amongst workers. They should be rejected, as should any attempt to reduce the civil wars in ex-Yugoslavia to the suffering of the Muslims. This is single issue politics of the worst kind. Its advocates have moved from uncritically supporting Tudjman against Milosevic to now trying to insulate Izetbegovic from the kind of criticisms that many ordinary Muslims are beginning to voice.

The act of conscience salving that is involved in calling for the arming of the Muslims does not begin to deal with the oppression of the Muslims of the Sandzak, the Hungarians and Croats of Vojvodina, the Serbs of the Croatian cities, the Albanians of Kosovo, or even with the question of Macedonia. This is especially important. If a Balkan civil war breaks out over the right of self determination of Macedonia, pulling in Serbia, Bulgaria, Greece, Albania and Turkey, it will be both impossible and reactionary to look for good guys and bad guys.

The only politics adequate to the dynamic of events is one which argues that the national rights of all peoples can only be secured by the workers of the region uniting against their common oppressors to forge a socialist federation of the Balkans. This is the only way forward. We should not turn our backs on it.

Chapter 11

Powers of partition

A new round of Western military intervention and diplomatic manoeuvring in Bosnia has produced nothing but embarrassment for the Western powers and still less hope for those suffering the carnage of war.

Many hoped that the deal which forced the Bosnian government into a new alliance with the Croatian forces in February would herald the beginning of the end for the fighting. This deal was very much the result of US pressure. United Nations threats followed by Russian manoeuvres then seemed to bring hope to many of the main cities under siege including the capital, Sarajevo. Commentators then talked of bringing Serbia into an extended deal which may lay the basis for an end to the war.

However, the UN soon found that military intervention meant picking sides—against Serbia. The test came over Gorazde, a mainly Muslim city (and a UN safe haven). On 10 and 11 April President Bill Clinton sanctioned the first ever NATO air to ground attacks against the Serbian forces laying close siege to the city. No sooner were the attacks launched, however, than they were stopped. The Western leaders then rapidly shifted their attention to the possibility of a new deal with Serbia. Clinton covered his gyration by claiming he had merely responded to a 'technical request'. Yet soon after the attack the US government said it was willing to consider a French proposal to discuss lifting international sanctions against Serbia.

For those who had hoped Western military intervention would provide a solution in Bosnia—including most of the British left— these events must seem frustrating and confusing.

One reason for the about face was that the episode highlighted the weakness of the Western powers, and confirmed the fears of those in the military establishment who dread getting bogged down in Bosnia. After the air strikes the situation soon turned messy for the West as UN aircraft were shot down, and UN forces came under attack and

First published May 1994

were taken hostage. An SAS unit sent to Gorazde in advance of the air strikes 'beat a stealthy retreat, leaving their United Nations High Commission for Refugees colleagues without saying a word'. If that were not embarrassing enough, these events took place as the US shot down its own helicopters over northern Iraq. The on-off attack of Gorazde also illustrates the military frictions between the Western powers. The British and French governments would dearly like the US to commit ground troops. Clinton, however, has been adamant against this. According to one NATO source, 'There is no clear sign of the will to act militarily in the [alliance] capitals.'

The events also reflect the relationship between the US and Russia. The US has been keen to both assert its independent power, but at the same time keep Russia on board as the possible broker of a deal with Serbia. This pattern was also shown clearly in the brinkmanship that accompanied the partial lifting of the siege of Sarajevo.

The response by many liberal commentators to the actions of the last month has been predictable—to argue that more firepower should be used against Serbia. This was also the position of Labour's Jack Cunningham. But arguing this position not only ignores the weakness of the West in Bosnia. It also falls into the trap of plumping for one of the three possible ways in which the imperialist powers might attempt to stitch Bosnia up.

The US government in particular has made faltering attempts to resolve the conflict by coming in decisively on the side of the Bosnian Croats and Muslims—this was clearly the intention of the Muslim-Croat pact they pushed through earlier in the year. But the Bosnian Croat, and more recently Bosnian Muslim, authorities have carried out the atrocities of ethnic cleansing every bit as zealously as the Bosnian Serbs.

Another option is to lift the arms embargo. But this would flood the country, with more arms going to all three sides in the battle, and be an open invitation to those governments, such as Turkey, which want to step up and broaden the conflict for their own ends.

The other alternative, now being considered by the US in particular, is to end aid operations and increase pressure for all sides to agree a final ethnic partition of the country. This has been the effective aim of all Western intervention throughout the war. Even the recent Muslim-Croat agreement, for example, was hailed by one US official as 'a sophisticated division of the Bosnian republic between Croatia and Serbia'.

Indeed, the fighting around Gorazde can be seen as a Serbian attempt to get the maximum out of a carve up that has already been agreed, 'cleansing' one of the last Muslim outposts on 'their' side of the country.

We cannot tell which of these options will be backed. The war in Bosnia is characterised by the acutest instability. We do know, however, that the war is an attempt by the leaders of Serbia, Croatia, Bosnia and the major powers to ride out the storm created by the economic and political collapse of the former Yugoslavia.

The Western military presence there has not stopped a single atrocity, and the Western attacks against the Serbs have only succeeded in driving ordinary Serbs back into supporting their leaders. Indeed, Western intervention is undermining those who attempt to bring real solace to the victims of war. Cornelio Sammaruga, president of the International Red Cross, has complained that the military presence 'undermines the humanitarian aid effort'.

As we have long argued, the only hope lies with those who have nothing to gain from war and ethnic partition—the ordinary people on all sides. They have struck, mutinied, demonstrated and deserted against both the war and its effects. Three years of Western intervention, pressing them to back their own leaders and ethnic partition, have only held them back.

Chapter 12

War without end?

Duncan Blackie

The war in Bosnia has been relaunched with a vengeance. There were widespread hopes this spring that negotiated deals could lead to a permanent end to fighting. But the prospects of peace were shattered by a series of events which may yet launch the war on its most dangerous phase.

The latest crisis was sparked in May as the contending sides faced the choice of extending a three month ceasefire or starting new military offensives. Muslim and Croatian forces tried to seize back land taken by the Serbians at the start of the war. The Serbians responded by moving heavy weapons back into areas from which they were excluded by UN rules.

On 25 and 26 May NATO jets attacked Serbian positions. What followed showed the folly of and the limits to Western intervention, as 300 UN soldiers were taken hostage by the Serbians and about 70 people were killed in Serbian bombardments of Muslim 'safe areas' such as Tuzla.

Then in June the Bosnian government started its most ambitious offensive yet—to drive a wide corridor between Sarajevo and the main bulk of Bosnian held territory. These events have thrown the debate about Bosnia once more onto centre stage. Western leaders are in turmoil over whether to stay—under the guise of the UN—to go, or to move in even greater numbers of troops. On the left there are renewed calls from many for the Western powers to stop pussyfooting around and sort out the 'Serb aggressors'. It is time, they say, for the left to clearly take the side of the 'just'—the Bosnians.

With fighting in the former Yugoslavia now having lasted as long as the First World War, there is a justifiable feeling of frustration. However, the latest events, far from showing the need for renewed intervention, have shown the folly of supporting either increased Western

First published July 1995

intervention, or of supporting one side in the conflict.

Socialist Review has throughout argued two things about the conflict in the former Yugoslavia.

The first is that it is pointless to view the war in terms of 'good' and 'bad' sides. The war in Bosnia was started largely as the result of an agreement struck between Serbian leader Slobodan Milosevic and Croatian leader Franjo Tudjman that they should carve up the territory between them. Both the Serbian and the Croatian leaderships whipped up ethnic hatred against others in order to deflect attention from the chronic political and economic crises wracking their countries.

Croatian forces overrunning Western Slavonia (a traditionally Serbian populated area of Croatia) this spring ejected civilians from their homes just as ruthlessly as Serbian forces have done to others (or as Croatian forces have been doing for the last four years).

The battle for the former Yugoslavia has therefore been characterised by a cynical battle between ruling groups with two aims in mind: to grab as much territory as possible and, in doing so, to stir ethnic hatred against ordinary people from different backgrounds. This factor would have only a tenth of the impact were it not for the fact that every nationality can point to wrongs done to its own people, which therefore reinforces grudging identification with rulers who argue that only an ethnically based solution is possible.

Many who brand Serbia as the sole aggressor will now admit, however, that the Croatian leadership has been culpable too. But, they say, the side of the Bosnian Muslims is different. They have been bullied by the major powers of the former Yugoslavia and systematically neglected by the Western powers.

Many may feel that the Bosnians have been singled out for persecution as they are Muslims. This can certainly seem a powerful argument in the context of countries like Britain where anti-Muslim bigotry serves as the umbrella of respectable and less respectable racism. Internationally, imperialism seems to have a track record of singling out Muslims.

However, the argument does not in reality hold water, and it is quite wrong to portray the war in Bosnia as the struggle of oppressed against oppressors. The Muslims of Bosnia were not an oppressed group before the war started. Their occupation of senior positions was largely in proportion to their numbers and they could not be shown to suffer disproportionately on any economic index. Indeed, in cities like Sarajevo, and particularly among the young, identification with a Serb, Croat or Muslim background was considered irrelevant to modern concerns.

Since the war started, the official Bosnian leadership has progressively come to mimic those of Serbia and Croatia. It is true they were the last to be drawn into the conflict, and lasted longer than any others as a multi-ethnic entity (there are still Serbs and Croats in the government). However, the government under Alia Izetbegovic has had to turn to ethnically based solutions in the absence of a class based alternative. By turns, the Bosnian leadership has found itself in alliance with Croatia, accepting Western demands for a solution based on separation, and then, from the end of 1993, combining both these policies with Muslim ethnic chauvinism to carve out the greatest possible slice of territory with offensives in central Bosnia.

Izetbegovic has been described by the very sympathetic journalist Ed Vulliamy as 'a man who had embraced the ethnicisation of politics as eagerly as any of his contemporaries'. Even in spring 1992 Izetbegovic had endorsed, with the Croatian and Serbian leaders, a plan to ethnically partition Bosnia. Only an outcry in Sarajevo forced him to reverse his plan.

The Bosnian government was then in alliance with Croatia. Yet this broke down with the first joint victories over Serbian forces. Just as the Serbian seige of Mostar was collapsing in the spring of 1992, Bosnian Serb and Croat leaders met in Graz to divide the country between themselves. Still Izetbegovic clung to his 'alliance', and the key Western diplomats of the time, Cyrus Vance and David Owen, 'endorsed the wilder claims of "Herceg-Bosnia" [the Croats' planned separate state]…giving the Croats not only Hercegovina, but country stretching deep into predominantly Muslim central Bosnia.' By the spring and summer of 1993 the 'alliance' was effectively dead. Now the Bosnian government stood on its own as a third power fighting for territory, and with no strategy other than an appeal to Muslim nationalism.

Misha Glenny wrote of the 'increasingly influential radical wing of President Izetbegovic's Party of Democratic Action (SDA) whose base in Zenica north of Sarajevo has become a centre of Muslim nationalism, and, it must be said, intolerance. The Zenica authorities were the first to undertake "cleansing"operations against Croats earlier this year'. He reported Muslim and Croatian forces fighting to make real the divisions suggested by Western leaders, characterised by the same horrors as those which had taken place in fighting between Serbs and Croats, and Serbs and Muslims.

Today the Bosnian government is back in alliance with the same

Croatian forces which threw 45,000 to 55,000 people out of their homes in Mostar alone. It is hard to see the Bosnian government forces as committed to a multi-ethnic solution merely because they are in league with ruthless ethnic cleansers of a different nationality.

There is much talk on the left of 'appeasement' and parallels made between the Bosnian war and the Spanish Civil War of the 1930s. They say that the procrastination of Western governments is akin to the 'non-intervention' of Britain and France in Spain which allowed fascist Germany and Italy to intervene unhampered on the side of the fascist forces.

But this is quite a different kind of war. In Spain the war was fought between, on the one hand, a Republican side of Communists, anarchists and liberals, and on the other hand, a nationalist side led by fascists. Franco aimed to annihilate working class organisation, while the Republicans fought to improve workers' conditions and, in the case of many anarchists and socialists, for the overthrow of capitalism.

How far this is from Bosnia where all sides—no matter what their differences in military strength or records of atrocities—are fighting for the control of territories in which the status quo will remain. Of course there are minor differences to be discerned, but the key questions that could make one side more progressive—such as even the promise of trade union rights or improved living standards—are on no leader's agenda.

Some people say that even if Izetbegovic is to be criticised, surely we can best do that while supporting the 'authentic' voice of Bosnian internationalism? The trouble is that this hardly exists, and where it does it comes under fire from the official leadership in Sarajevo.

The aims of the Bosnian leadership are objectively the same as the Serbian or Croatian leaderships, and support for the Bosnian side in no sense promotes class struggle. Instead it just involves the left in the quagmire of ethnic divisions without pointing the way forward.

This leads to the second thing *Socialist Review* has consistently argued—that the leaders of the major outside powers can provide no solution. We argued that the failure firstly of Russian-style 'state capitalism' and then of Western-style market capitalism lay at the root of economic collapse and political despair. The Western rulers have shown throughout that they can at best mirror the rotten policies of ex-Yugoslavia's own rulers. At worst, they can reproduce the tragedy on a higher and more terrible scale.

Hence round after round of proposed settlements—all of which have involved the division of the country on ethnic grounds. This is what lies at the heart of the West's dilemma.

We have seen the utter ineffectiveness of 'peacekeeping' in the regions where the UN is supposed to guarantee the peace. When assaults were launched on the Bosnian 'safe havens' last winter, the UN was incapable of stopping them. And when in May Serbian forces were ejected from Western Slavonia, a UN official told the *Economist*, 'We're certainly not going to stop the Croats. It's not what we've been asked to do, just as we are not going to stop the Serbs by use of force.'

The hostage crisis and the June offensive threw Western leaders into new levels of turmoil. President Clinton first talked tough, with hints of US ground troops being made available. This position was quickly reversed, however, and both the US and France settled for tough posturing about the possibility of heavier air attacks. The British government, meanwhile, merely despaired that its planned withdrawal of troops would have to be reversed, in the short term at least.

Western policy in Bosnia is slowly swinging round. The US in particular has pursued a twin track. On the one hand, it has tried to sever the links between the leadership of the Serbian state and its acolytes leading the fighting in Bosnia. This spring Milosevic promised to recognise the borders of Bosnia in return for a lifting of Western sanctions against Serbia.

On the other hand, the US in particular is moving to fulfil its long term goal of siding clearly with the Bosnian government. The more far sighted of US leaders, as well as 'isolationist' right wingers, are wary of this strategy, however, and talk in terms of crossing the 'Mogadishu line'—a reference to the disaster of the US fighting on one side of the civil war in Somalia.

Yet talk has resumed of lifting the arms boycott to the Bosnian government. This, plus the posturing which surrounded the hostage crisis, must surely be one of the factors behind the decision by Croatian and Muslim forces to launch the June offensive.

Even without an official lifting of the arms embargo, the Bosnian government hardly stands alone. Some of the most reactionary states in the world, including the Middle Eastern oil sheikhdoms, have provided arms. There are almost certainly arms covertly arriving in Bosnia from US sources.

Now, at the very least, Clinton envisages a strategy of combining arms shipments to the Bosnian government while providing air cover for offensives. Increased arms aid to a force already powerful beyond the rhetoric about 'poor little Bosnia' could make for a major difference on the ground. 'Even modest levels of targeted support from the West could significantly shift the balance of forces in Bosnia, without involvement of foreign ground troops', according to a director of the US Institute of Peace.

Others in the US ruling class have an interesting variant on this theme and talk of the need for the return of the 'Reagan Doctrine': using covert means to secure the aims of US power. The right wing chairman of the foreign relations committee, Jesse Helms, said the UN should 'begin treating the Bosnians as we did the [Nicaraguan] Contras'.

Western leaders have spent four years warning each other about the dangers of getting stuck in a quagmire. They are now stuck in one without even the option of a simple withdrawal. The present level of Western intervention has been capable of no more than sanctioning the repeated carve up of Bosnia. Increased levels of military involvement can only make matters worse by destabilising the whole region and drawing Western forces into a direct battle with the Serbs in particular.

The Western leaders' strategy in Bosnia has had terrible results. They sought to 'contain' the crisis and have succeeded in helping it rage on for four years. Those on the left who call for taking sides are stuck too. By turning their backs on what can unite ordinary people of all ethnic backgrounds—a class hatred of their leaders—they have had to side in despair with people following the very policies they despise.

There is an alternative, however, and it lies with all those people who have lost the most from the war. Workers in Belgrade and Zagreb (and Sarajevo too) have had their living standards and political freedom dashed by a war that has been fought to save the necks of those responsible for their misery.

It is not a pipe dream to hope that these resentments can turn into class struggle—they already have done in every year of the war. Even on the rural front lines, where the day to day demands of war are more immediate and there are fewer traditions of class struggle, new antagonisms threaten to undermine the militarists.

If such soldiers learned that ordinary Muslims hate their own leaders too, and the US air force which rains bombs on them, the trance of mutual fear could be broken. Those on the left who talk solely of the 'Serbian menace', however, are doing their bit to stop this coming true.

Chapter 13

Europe's bloody war

Lindsey German, Gareth Jenkins and Sabby Sagall

The summer months have seen a deadly turn in the course of the war in the former Yugoslavia. The picture painted only a couple of months ago was of besieged Muslims in the so called safe areas pounded by the Bosnian Serb aggressors.

Croatia's invasion of the Serb populated Krajina has changed all that, forcing up to 200,000 Krajina Serb refugees to flee to Bosnian Serb areas or even to Serbia, in a process described by the UN as the largest amount of ethnic cleansing since present hostilities began four years ago.

The real forces behind the war are becoming more obvious as time goes on. Croatia launched its invasion after making a formal military pact with Bosnia, and with the tacit agreement of Germany and especially the US. The US ambassador told Croatia's president Tudjman that the war had to be a 'short and clean battle', and the US was centrally involved in brokering the peace deal with Bosnia.

As the *Financial Times* reported:

> The US makes no attempt to disguise its support. When Mr Tudjman signed a military pact with his Bosnian counterpart, Mr Alia Izetbegovic, Mr Peter Galbraith, the US ambassador to Croatia, was included in the photograph. The ink was hardly dry on that agreement before thousands of Croat troops, infiltrated into Bosnia over the previous weeks, launched their attack in Western Bosnia. There was no protest from Washington or other Western capitals, and certainly no threat of air strikes on attacking Croat forces.

First published September 1995

The US Congress's decision to lift the Bosnian arms embargo and NATO's most recent use of air strikes against Bosnian Serbs have further fuelled the threat of all out war developing far beyond the borders of Bosnia.

The continued Western intervention plus the formal alliance between the two states of Croatia and Bosnia gives the lie to the two notions so beloved of the British media: that the Serbs are the sole aggressors in this war and that it is simply an internal dispute between different ethnic groups, of whom the Serbs are by far the worst.

In fact the war is about the repartition of the former Yugoslavia, where ethnic cleansing has been sanctioned by all the major powers and where it is practised by all three sides in the conflict. The victims of this bloody war—the dead, the orphaned, the refugees—are from every nationality.

Croatia is trying to take back land that it lost in 1991 when it declared its independence from Yugoslavia. The strongly nationalist Serb area of Krajina then resisted breaking away from Serbia, fearing the repressive Croat nationalist regime would discriminate against it. Since May, when Tudjman's forces invaded Western Slavonia, the attack on Krajina has been on the cards.

There is confidence among Croatia's rulers that the West will do nothing to stop its army running roughshod over the Serbs, despite the murmurs of protest at the invasion. As the *Independent* said:

> Croatia's armed forces have struck without incurring any censure from Western governments, most of which do not seem unhappy that the Krajina Serbs and their Bosnian Serb brethren are finally getting a taste of their own medicine. The most recent Croat offensive in Western Bosnia has been useful to the West in that it has relieved Serb pressure on the Muslim enclave of Bihac and has removed the sense of urgency over the divisive question of whether NATO should deter attacks on Bihac with air strikes.

The Western powers are hoping that repartition enforced by the Croats can stop the war in Bosnia—although at massive cost to the various populations. The cynicism of the outside powers is obvious. They are prepared to back ethnic cleansing and partition if it makes the area more 'stable'. But it is a very dangerous game for the West to play—a fact that Western leaders themselves are aware of. Hence the divisions between them, and the reluctance of particularly Britain and France to commit too many troops to the area.

It is all too possible that Serbia can be dragged into the war, especially if Eastern Slavonia, which borders Serbia, is attacked by Croatia. Tudjman has already said he will attack the region, thereby putting pressure on Serbia's Milosevic, who so far has left the Bosnian Serbs to sink.

A full scale war between Croatia and Serbia will not only be much more bloody than what we are seeing at present, but threatens to involve Russia on Serbia's side, increasingly unhappy with the US's role in backing Croatia and Bosnia. The likelihood of a full scale Balkan war, involving powers such as Greece and Turkey, is also greater than it was even a few months ago.

In such a situation it is very important that we understand what is at stake in this war and the attitude socialists should take. The war arose out of the collapse of the former Yugoslavia, when the ex-Communist leaders of Serbia and Croatia banged the nationalist drum in an attempt to divert discontent and strikes following the collapse of the economy. The independence of Croatia and Slovenia—backed by Germany and the rest of the EU—led directly to the war, with Serbia fearing a Croatian regime which used the symbols of the hated wartime pro-Nazi Ustashe, deliberately encouraged by Tudjman to bolster his support and win finance from right wing expatriate Croats.

Tudjman and Milosevic were happy to do a deal then to partition Bosnia between the two powers. Right from the start there was little to choose between the sides. Yet many on the left who now proclaim Bosnia the innocent victim took a similar view of Croatia in 1991. It was argued that Croatia was only acting defensively, was more democratic than Serbia and indulged in less ethnic cleansing.

Today this argument is hardly tenable, but the status of victim has now been transferred to the Muslims in Bosnia. However, just as taking the side of Croatia in 1991 ignored the wider issues and the various outside powers involved in the war, so the idea of the Bosnian Muslim government as the innocent party in all this succumbs to the worst sort of single issue politics and fails to understand what is really happening.

The Bosnian government is a major player in this war, and indeed launched the war's latest phase earlier this summer. The Bosnian army is an increasingly professional and well equipped army, receiving arms from Eastern Europe and Iran through Croatia, which takes its own cut. The backing for Bosnia by the Great Powers is increasingly strident, and its current alliance with Croatia gives it very substantial military forces.

It is claimed that the Bosnian government is more multi-ethnic, but this is becoming less the case as the war develops. The Bosnians have also been involved in ethnic cleansing, for example in Zenica against the local Croats. According to a Dutch UN commander in Srebrenica, 'Bosnian Muslims had burned around 200 surrounding villages' in July.

The nature of the war makes it inevitable that the misery and atrocities inflicted on one group of people will be reproduced against other groups. This is the hideous logic which has been at work, and which now sees Krajina Serbs fleeing in large numbers from the advancing Croatian forces. It is inevitable that we will continue to see Serbs, Croats and Muslims at different times both as aggressors and victims in the war.

Any war of partition has this effect, as different nationalities are removed over often quite arbitrary boundaries. In Bosnia, where a third of the pre-war population was Serb and a fifth Croat, all sides will be involved in the forcible removal of populations.

The point here is not to take sides but to argue for a solution not based on intervention from the West, which can only make the situation much worse and will do nothing to help the beleaguered populations. Rather it is to say that the solution lies with the peoples of the region themselves. If they want to end the war, they have to begin to present a challenge to all their nationalist leaders which can begin to point the way to a peaceful—multi-ethnic—solution.

Looking for the good guys

Faced with carnage in the Balkans, many on the left have seen no other possibility but to take sides. A handful, out of distrust of Western anti-Serbian propaganda, have sided with Serbia, and a few around Tony Benn oppose Western intervention (though he too is prepared to share platforms with pro-Serbia anti-interventionists). But the vast majority have become cheerleaders for Bosnia.

The result has been to put them in the same camp as the right wing critics of the British and US governments. The pro-Bosnia section of the left has joined hands with the ultra-imperialists who want to increase Western military intervention in the Balkans. This capitulation to the idea that tough action is needed to face down reactionary powers first surfaced during the Gulf War, when a section of the left saw Saddam Hussein's regime as qualitatively worse than bourgeois democracy and drew the conclusion that the US might have a progressive role to play. Now the argument found in publications like the *Guardian* and the *New Statesman* is that Serbia is a fascist power getting away with aggression because democrats are failing to defend Bosnia.

The comparison is with the 1930s. The Western European powers, dithering and impotent, are like the appeasers who failed to intervene to prevent the spread of Hitlerism across Europe. Unless Serbia is stopped now, a similar catastrophe will begin to unfold. Those who oppose intervention are complicit with the appeasers or, even worse, with Serbian fascism.

Thus former Labour Party leader Michael Foot brands Bosnia 'the great anti-fascist war of your generation'. Left wing MP Callum MacDonald sees Bosnia as 'Spain, Abyssinia and Czechoslovakia rolled into one. It is as clear to me how the left should react, as it was to Hitlerism in the 1930s'. Ed Vulliamy endorsed these sentiments in the *Guardian* in mid-July using a tone bordering on the apocalyptic:

> If we thought that the defeat of the Third Reich meant that the bullies of history need not triumph in Europe, we were wrong. But one dividing line persists: between those who believe in defying the evils, and those who shrug or smudge the horrors with words.

These evils are 'comparable to the worst horrors of the Holocaust itself', argued Michael Foot, this time from the platform of a 1,500 strong meeting called by the Alliance to Defend Bosnia-Hercegovina in late July. The Bosnian ambassador in London painted a larger picture of barbarism: 'If the Serb fascists win, tomorrow it will be the Russian fascists.'

It follows, therefore, as another speaker put it, that the defence of Bosnia is no local matter: 'The Bosnian army is fighting for civilisation and culture.' Vulliamy reinforced the idea: 'None of this need have happened. Bosnia is being destroyed in a drunken Gestapo way. The future of Bosnia is the yardstick of how to judge this civilisation.'

These are emotional statements. Nonetheless the argument is false. The idea that what is happening in Bosnia is like the Holocaust is to trivialise both the scale of what happened in the Nazi death camps and what they tell us about a truly fascist regime.

The systematic murder of six million Jews by production line methods is what gives the Holocaust its uniqueness in comparison with the mass killings which occur in any large scale and long lasting civil war. It took place in an advanced, heavily industrialised country whose ruling class resorted to the use of a mass movement to smash working class organisation.

Serbia bears no resemblance. It is not in the same economic league as Nazi Germany, nor can one point to a mass fascist movement of the type which characterised Nazi Germany.

Under Hitler there were no independent working class organisations. Serbia possesses trade unions with sufficient independence to have organised a general strike over wages only three years ago.

In addition, Bosnia cannot be compared to the pre-war victims of fascism, least of all to Spain. The civil war in Spain was at bottom a class war, with the bulk of the bourgeoisie lining up behind Franco, and the mass of the working class and peasantry defending their control of the land and the factories within the republic. No such seizure of land or factories has occurred in Bosnia.

If Bosnia is no Spain, perhaps it is an Abyssinia or a Czechoslovakia, with a right to self defence? Again, the comparison does not hold. The right to self defence is fine so long as that country does not become a pawn of imperialist intervention. Bosnia's existence cannot now be disentangled from the interests of imperialism.

Bosnia is allied to Croatia, which has been given *carte blanche* by the US to drive Serbs out of their homes in Krajina. To champion Bosnia's right to self defence in the abstract is simply to legitimate the whole ghastly process and to line up, once again, with the most reactionary elements of Western imperialism.

The tragedy of the civil war in Bosnia is that there are no class differences between the Serbs and the Muslims; its bitterness derives from the fact that both sides marshal the same people under rival national flags. Between these rival nationalisms there is no essential difference. To support Bosnia on the grounds that we are defending a 'progressive' cause is a grotesque travesty of the truth.

But it is worse than that. For the idea that we are involved in an anti-fascist crusade is also wrapped up in the idea that we should invoke intervention, no matter what the nature of that intervention, and should ally ourselves with anyone, no matter how reactionary. As the left wing weekly *Tribune* put it, 'Even Margaret Thatcher can be right sometimes, and on this issue she is.' Time and time again the appeal to do something about the situation is couched in terms of the need to restore the credibility of the UN or the moral authority of NATO.

It is argued that the only problem with these bodies is that they have failed to act, and so betrayed the trust of small nations. But this is to assume that their purpose is to keep the peace. Nothing, of course, could be further from the truth. Both the UN and NATO exist to preserve the imperialist world order. The 'indecisiveness' of the UN reflects not a reluctance to intervene but splits and tensions between the world's ruling classes as to how to intervene.

The contradiction they face is this: they feel that if they do not intervene the conflict will spill over and affect much more vital interests, chiefly in the Middle East. But they can not intervene too directly for fear of being sucked into a land war with unacceptable casualty rates.

Up until now they have more or less accepted the idea of political diplomacy to get the different sides themselves to regularise ethnic cleansing (the various plans to divide Bosnia), with troops being no more than a backup.

Now the balance is being tipped (by an increasingly influential section of the US ruling class) in favour of a different option. They hope that a combination of NATO air power and a rearmed Bosnian army can provide the military muscle for a solution without having Western troops bogged down in a Vietnam-style quagmire. None of this resolves the other problem of containing the conflict once the ever leakier arms embargo is ended.

This phase of imperialist meddling inevitably means greater and not less bloodshed. In the Gulf War 'precision bombing' by the US of Iraqi military targets resulted in thousands of civilian casualties—and that was in a sparsely populated and easily observable desert terrain. How can it be any more precise in the context of a very different country like the former Yugoslavia—especially if NATO decides to aim its bombs at large cities like Belgrade?

By supporting intervention the left will be powerless to stop ever more reactionary forms of nationalism appearing. It will also find itself on the opposite side to those in the anti-war movement who want to combat nationalism.

A foretaste of that came in the meeting of the Alliance to Defend Bosnia-Hercegovina, at which Michael Foot and Ed Vulliamy spoke, when a message from Serbian anti-war protesters in Belgrade was jeered by a good third of the audience.

Those who have called for workers' aid to defend a 'multi-ethnic' Bosnia are in reality backing such reactionary nationalism. Some have openly endorsed anti-Serb chauvinism.

It is not the job of the left to find reasons to encourage intervention. It is our job to say no to such intervention, however much dressed up in democratic garb, and yes to each and every element of class resistance to all the nationalisms of the region.

Reluctant soldiers

From the outbreak of war in the former Yugoslavia in 1991 anti-war movements arose. In Belgrade in March 1991 tens of thousands of students and workers marched against repression and for democracy. The high point of a week of mass action saw half a million people occupy the city centre. The Centre for Anti-War Action was established in July. It organised demonstrations, rock concerts and it led a march for peace around the Yugoslav parliament. In April 1992, after the war had spread to Bosnia, it organised a demonstration opposing it, and 100,000 participated in a concert proclaiming, 'Don't count on us.'

In 1993 some 1,500 people took part in a demonstration in Belgrade marking the first anniversary of the siege of Sarajevo. Serbian television denounced the protesters as traitors. A bi-monthly magazine, *Republika*, was published with a circulation of 5,000, as well as leaflets, posters, advertisements and general media publicity, aimed mainly at students and intellectuals. The aim of all these activities was to mobilise against the war and to send a message of solidarity to all those resisting it.

The Anti-War Campaign of Croatia was also founded in 1991 when hostilities in the Slavonia and Krajina regions of Croatia were in full swing. It too published a bi-monthly magazine, *Arkzin*, which continues to report on anti-war initiatives. It campaigns for the rights of conscientious objectors and defends Serbs thrown out of their homes by right wing Croatian militias.

There have been significant workers' actions against the effects of the war in both Serbia and Croatia. In Serbia in July 1993 thousands of workers went on strike demanding payment of wages owed: 18,000 miners, 10,000 chemical workers and also engineers. In August 1993 it was estimated that 10 percent of Serbian industry was on strike at any one time.

In Croatia in March 1993 there was a half hour general strike, called by the Independent Trade Unions, a warning to the government to take note of collapsing living standards. It was supported by 50 percent of the workforce and resulted in Croatian president Tudjman dismissing his government. Journalists and printers on the paper *Slobodna Dalmacija* went on strike against a takeover by the state.

Meanwhile, unemployment continues to rise, the rate now standing at 18 percent. The 1995 military budget will consume 41 percent of government expenditure. Recently, there have been a number of short isolated strikes, also over non-payment of wages, particularly among textile and shipbuilding workers.

In May 1992 the UN Security Council imposed economic sanctions against Serbia. In January 1994 hyper-inflation was running at a daily rate of 97 percent. There are severe shortages of food, fuel and medicines, a rapidly falling currency and a 50 percent unemployment rate. Half the country's industrial capacity remains idle and nearly a million workers in Serbia and Montenegro are on 'compulsory holiday'.

A further indication of the growing unpopularity of the war has been the increasing rate of desertion and draft dodging among Bosnian Serbs. A recent report by the Institute for European Strategic and Defence Studies quotes Yugoslavian army sources criticising the flight of military age Serbs from safe areas in Bosnia. By early 1993 at least 53,000 registered, and many more unregistered, draft age Serbs from Bosnia and Croatia had moved to Serbia, despite intensifying pressure on them to take up arms. By the autumn of 1993 the Bosnian Serb military courts had issued some 2,500 warrants for desertion.

It was recently reported that up to 60,000 military age men have fled to Montenegro. In Banja Luka in September 1993 there was a mutiny when 1,000 armed soldiers took control of the town and arrested the local clique. They demanded a crackdown on war profiteering, improved welfare for soldiers and their families, and immediate elections. The rebellion struck a chord with townspeople and local trade unionists. The rebels received many messages of support from other Bosnian Serb regions.

Large scale anti-war movements have often begun with small groups voicing opposition on a purely pacifist basis. The current military escalation is likely to intensify war weariness to the point where a revival of anti-war activity could connect with the economic misery felt by the mass of ordinary people.

Chapter 14

What a carve up

Lindsey German

A new and much more deadly horror came to the Balkans last month. Its creator was the NATO powers, who by unleashing their air strikes and cruise missiles against the Bosnian Serbs ensured even greater ethnic cleansing as thousands of Serb refugees fled from the offensive of the Bosnian and Croatian governments. The aim of the air strikes was to decisively weaken the Bosnian Serbs to ensure the ground offensive would be a success.

The action smacks strongly of the tactics employed during the Gulf War against Saddam Hussein in 1991, where superior Western air power meant the outcome of ground battles was made much more certain. And—as was the case with the Gulf War—such intervention created much greater atrocities than the ones it was supposedly dealing with.

Those on the left who have repeatedly called for such intervention should reflect on what the outcome already is. The numbers of Bosnian Serb refugees are now estimated at over 250,000, making it the biggest movement of population in Europe since the Second World War.

Whole swathes of Bosnia—as well as the historic Serb region of the Krajina—have now been totally ethnically cleansed of Serbs. The *Independent* journalist Robert Fisk has filed numerous reports of atrocities against Krajina Serbs. Many of the older Serbs, unable to flee, have been murdered, their houses looted and burned.

All this is ensuring that multi-ethnicity is a thing of the past in much of the former Yugoslavia. The Western powers may throw up their hands in horror at the worst extremes now taking place against the displaced Serbs, but they have been willing to turn a blind eye to many of the atrocities. Indeed, the US brokered the current military alliance between the Croatian state and the Bosnian government.

First published October 1995

The US ambassador to Croatia, Peter Galbraith, has referred to the Krajina Serbs—who have lived in the region for 400 years—as 'so called local Serbs', thus encouraging the idea that they should be driven out of the region.

The Bosnian government—still hailed by many on the left as an example of multi-ethnicity and peaceful intent—has shown in recent weeks that its past restraint had more to do with relative military weakness than anything else. And the Bosnian state itself is becoming much less ethnically diverse as the war progresses. As the *Economist* said recently:

> Many of the liberal intellectuals who championed a multi-ethnic society have left Bosnia. An influx of refugees from rural areas, many of them religious, has helped to marginalise the Croats and Serbs who live on Bosnian government territory...only Muslims belonging to the SDA stand a chance of rising high in the administration, army, media or business world.

The outcome of the 'peace talks' is still unclear, but the signs are that Croatia and Bosnia are holding out for more land than the US originally wanted to give them. In addition, the Bosnian government is insisting that Bosnian Serbs cannot secede, even though that is clearly the wish of many. The proposed carve up will only reinforce the ethnic divisions which exist. The Bosnian Muslims will also find themselves under pressure from their allies who want a Greater Croatia.

Croatian president Franjo Tudjman is threatening to take Eastern Slavonia, which joins directly onto Serbia, and the Bosnian government is talking of invading Banja Luka, where tens of thousands of Serb refugees have taken shelter. This will only result in further bloodshed and ethnic cleansing.

Serbian president Slobodan Milosevic has so far done little to help the Bosnian Serbs, preferring to compromise with the Western powers. But further invasion and ethnic cleansing puts even greater pressure on him to intervene, especially if Croatia fights in Eastern Slavonia.

So far the balance sheet of the Western backed Croatian-Bosnian offensive, plus the air strikes, has been to bring a much bloodier war to the region and make it harder for the ordinary people of whatever nationality to live in peace.

The culprits in this are the Western powers, who have used the region for their own cynical ends. Those who urge intervention for peace by force should reflect that this has brought us a more deadly war.

Chapter 15

The Balkan war: can there be peace?

Lindsey German

At a banquet in London last May Croatian president Franjo Tudj-man drew a sketch on the back of his menu card. It was a map of Bosnia as he predicted it would look in ten years time, partitioned between Serbia and Croatia. The dinner gathered together various heads of state and other dignitaries to celebrate the fiftieth anniver-sary of VE Day (to which Tudjman was invited despite his pro-fascist sympathies). Few of them—including Tudjman himself—could have predicted that the war in the former Yugoslavia was about to take so dramatic a turn against the Bosnian Serbs, and that only months later the sketch map would bear a much closer resemblance to reality.

Events in the former Yugoslavia have moved so fast in recent months that the balance of forces in the region has changed completely. Calls for Western intervention and for arming the Bosnian government have been heeded by the US and its allies with predictably bloody conse-quences. The relative weakness of the Bosnian government's military forces has been largely overcome by NATO air strikes which destroyed many of the Bosnian Serb defences. The displacement of the Krajina Serbs and Bosnian Serbs represents the biggest movement of refugees in Europe since the Second World War. There are more and more sto-ries of atrocities against Serbs, although most of them tend to get very little publicity in the Western media, in strong contrast to the stories of atrocities committed by Serbs against Muslims or Croats.

The Serb nationalists' dreams of a Greater Serbia have turned to nothing as Serbs have been ethnically cleansed from whole swathes of Bosnia and Krajina. The Serbian government has not lifted a finger to help them.

First published winter 1995

The shift in the balance of forces has led to the latest peace plan, brokered by the US and cementing the current ethnic partition of the region. The peace deal allows a state which is 51 percent Muslim-Croatian federation and 49 percent Serbian. But there is little doubt which state will be dominant in the federation. As the *Economist* puts it, 'Mr Tudjman can probably have his cake and eat it: he can win Western plaudits for backing the Bosnian federation, knowing that despite its nominal independence and multi-ethnic constitution, it is likely to consist of little more than a Muslim statelet and a Croat statelet, and to be dependent on Croatia itself'.[1]

The reversal of Tudjman's fortunes has been made possible by one crucial element: the intervention of the Western powers, especially the US. The latest phase of the war has quite clearly seen Bosnian and Croatian forces on the ground moving in step with the wishes of the US. The Bosnian government offensive to drive a wide corridor between Sarajevo and most Bosnian territory, and Croatia's attack on Western Slavonia have both taken place alongside increased NATO intervention. So NATO jets attacked Serbian positions at the end of May shortly before the Bosnian government launched its offensive. The Croatian invasion of the Serb area of Krajina—called Operation Storm, recalling the Desert Storm invasion during the Gulf War—began soon after the conclusion of a military pact between the Croatian and Bosnian governments which was witnessed by the US ambassador to Croatia, Peter Galbraith. The September Croatian-Bosnian offensive against large chunks of Bosnian Serb territory was greatly helped by the destruction of the Bosnian Serb 'nervous system'—their defences and ammunition dumps—by NATO air strikes.

Despite much talk heralding peace, the most likely outcome is still instability and war, leading to misery for the vast majority of ordinary people of every nationality who have to live in the hell that the various republics have become. One journalist compared the current situation in Eastern Slavonia (which borders Serbia proper and which Tudjman has made noises about invading) with the situation just before war broke out in 1991:

> [War in Eastern Slavonia] will seem as certain as the war of 1991 seemed more than four years ago, when politicians crowed about peace and distraught villagers waited for war.[2]

The resurgence of Croatian and Bosnian government forces and the decisive intervention of the US have vindicated those who argued that this is a war in which socialists should not take sides. It is a war of repartition which, by definition, will discriminate in turn against different sections of the population simply because of their ethnic origin. In such circumstances the intervention of the Western imperialist powers can only make things worse. The events of recent months have borne out this view. However, there are many on the left who almost wilfully ignore recent developments, preferring to continue to paint the Serbs as 'fascist aggressors', and the Muslims, and to a lesser extent Croats, as innocent victims. Taking such a view means accepting fairly uncritically many of the nationalist views of the Croatian and Bosnian governments.[3]

So the recent suffering of the Krajina Serbs and many Bosnian Serbs has left many people cold. The *Independent's* editorial for 7 August, after Tudjman's *blitzkrieg* victory in the Krajina, began:

> It is tempting to feel euphoric about this weekend's Serbian defeat at the hands of the Croats. At last, the Serbs have been taught an overdue lesson, given a dose of the medicine that they have so freely administered in recent weeks to Bosnia's Muslims.[4]

Former Labour Party leader Michael Foot wrote three weeks after the invasion, 'The idea that the Croatian authorities were suddenly themselves adopting a policy of ethnic cleansing was a wicked lie'.[5]

Some liberals and left wingers have always seen the Muslims as the victims in this war. Indeed, some of them have even seen Croatia as the underdog. 'Serb aggression' has been blamed on the whole Serb population rather than on the nationalist military and political leaders. Such politics leave their advocates disarmed in the face of the many reports of atrocities in Krajina and the Bosnian Serb areas in recent months, and of a refugee problem on a massive scale with an estimated 250,000 Serbs on the move since August, and without any sense of a solution to the war.

'Siding with the victim' should in logic now lead such people to demonstrate some sympathy and support for the Bosnian Serbs. Instead, much 'respectable' liberal opinion is prepared to turn a blind eye to atrocities and injustices, including some of the worst ethnic cleansing of the war.

Yet now, more than ever, it is becoming apparent that there can be no winners apart from the nationalist leaders, the ruling classes who back them and the imperialist powers. The losers are those, from whatever background, who favour democracy, multi-ethnicity or any form of socialist solution to the problems of the region.

The invasion of Krajina

The latest phase of the war began last May when Muslim and Croatian forces started new military offensives in order to seize back land which Serbia took at the beginning of the war four years ago. The Croatian invasion of Western Slavonia in May was in many ways a dress rehearsal for the invasion of Krajina in August. In June the Bosnian government went on the offensive in order to ensure a corridor of land between most of its territories and Sarajevo. Then came the Muslim-Croat military pact, midwife to the Croatian army's invasion of the Krajina.

Krajina means, literally, frontier—the buffer zone on the edge of the old Austro-Hungarian Empire peopled by Serbs who had traditionally backed the Austrians against the Ottoman Empire. Today the area and its main town of Knin are strategically important to Croatia, lying between the capital, Zagreb, and the coastal resorts. The Serb dominated area wanted to remain with the former Yugoslavia when Croatia declared independence in 1991. The invasion this summer was to destroy the Serb republic of Krajina and to drive the vast majority of its Serb inhabitants to flee either to Bosnian Serb territory or to Serbia itself, as they feared (accurately) that the war would follow them east and northwards. The traditional Serb population in this Serb dominated area of Croatia were turned out of homes and farms. The invasion was completed within days, with devastating consequences. An estimated 150,000 Krajina Serbs were on the move in front of the advancing armies. The effect of the military pact between Croatia and Bosnia became clear: the invasion allowed the Muslims to break the siege of the Bihac pocket in north western Bosnia, while Croatia went ahead with its offensive.

The Croatian army recaptured a Serb dominated area populated by Serbs for over 300 years. Krajina Serbs were forced out through a campaign of atrocities which led to the biggest single displacement of a population during the war. Serb villages were looted and burned, farm livestock was killed and there were many instances of killings of older Serbs and anyone else who was left in the area. The motives of the Croatian army were clear. The *Washington Post* reported that 'human rights observers said the burning of homes and killing of livestock are designed to dissuade Serb refugees from returning'.[6] A UN spokesman was reported as saying two weeks after the invasion, 'Krajina is literally ablaze. There are villages which were turned into a living hell by the Croatian army. We have lists of villages where as many as 80 percent of the homes were torched.' Another observer said that an estimated 80 percent of buildings in the Knin area of Krajina had been damaged 'by organised burning and looting' on the part of the Croatian army and civilian police.[7]

The reaction of the Western media, echoing their rulers in the respective countries, has been to turn their backs on such atrocities. There have been no calls for air strikes against Croatia, no indicting of Tudjman or his generals for war crimes against a civilian population (unlike the treatment meted out to the Bosnian Serbs), and, indeed, a denial that many of the worst atrocities have even taken place. As the *Economist* commented ironically just after the invasion:

> Since the Croats did not load Serbs onto buses at gunpoint, as the Serbs themselves did to Muslims when they overran the eastern enclaves last month, the Croats argue that this is not ethnic cleansing, but flight. To the Krajina Serbs, who feared that their throats would be cut if they stayed, the distinction is not clear.[8]

The Krajina Serbs were right to fear for their lives. The Croatian authorities have denied looting, pillaging and killings by their troops, blaming any atrocity which is backed by hard evidence on 'uncontrolled elements', but eyewitnesses on the ground tell a different story. Within days of the Croatian army victory, civilian Croats driving cars with Zagreb number plates were seen looting empty homes near Glina in Krajina.[9] Serbs were not only driven out of areas which had been their home for generations, but signs were changed from the Cyrillic (Serbian) script to the Latin (Croatian) one, and Orthodox churches were destroyed.

Reports coming out of Krajina rapidly demonstrated that even worse events were taking place. The journalist Robert Fisk filed a series of reports in the *Independent* which are notable for their honesty. His reports paint a devastating picture of ethnic cleansing fuelled by sheer terror. For example, Fisk reported on 4 September 1995 how every house in the town of Kistanje had been destroyed by the Croatian army. He quotes a confidential document from the EU assessing the situation in the region which, as he says, speaks for itself:

> Evidence of atrocities, an average of six corpses per day, continues to

emerge...the corpses, some fresh, some decomposed, are mainly of old men. Many have been shot in the back of the head or had throats slit, others have been mutilated. Isolated pockets of elderly civilians report people recently gone missing or detained... Endless [Croat] invitations for Serbs to return, guarantees of citizens' rights and property rights etc, have gushed forth from all levels... However, Serbian homes and lands continue to be torched and looted.

Contrary to official statements blaming it on fleeing Serbs and uncontrollable elements, the crimes have been perpetrated by the HV [Croatian army], the CR [Croatian] police and CR civilians. There have been no observed attempts to stop it and the indications point to a scorched earth policy.[10]

Fisk also records a UN report which details the deaths of a whole number of elderly Serbs in Krajina, and his personal encounter with three Croatian soldiers who were engaged in burning and looting a Serb farmhouse.[11]

The invasion of Krajina marked a turning point. It began the offensive which spread throughout western Bosnia displacing tens of thousands more Serbs, thus putting the Croatian and Bosnian government forces clearly at an advantage in any subsequent carve up of land.

The incredible speed with which the Croatian forces took Krajina gave the military and the politicians the confidence and the impetus to go further. The Croatian and Bosnian military launched the attack on the Serbian held lands of western Bosnia, thereby setting about redrawing the boundaries of the Bosnian republic. They achieved by force in a matter of weeks more than had been achieved in the previous year.

But none of this would have been possible without the NATO air strikes. The combined Croatian and Bosnian Muslim armies far outnumbered the Bosnian Serbs even before this latest offensive, with an estimated 65,000 active troops plus another 15,000 reserves in the Bosnian Serb army, while the Croatian army alone has 105,000 active troops and 120,000 reserves, and the Bosnian Muslims another 160,000. The Bosnian Serbs have traditionally been better equipped—although they are now matched by the Croatians in many areas and outgunned by the combined weaponry of the two allied armies. US mercenaries have been used to train Bosnian troops in a 'boot camp' for the army. The Croatian army also receives training from a US firm, Military Professional Resources of Virginia, which sends retired

US army officers to teach at the Zagreb military academy.[12]

The NATO bombing was decisive in establishing the dominance of an already numerically superior force, with increasingly good training and better equipment, by wiping out their enemy's defensive equipment. NATO launched its air strikes in early September following the shelling of Sarajevo by Bosnian Serb artillery. This provided the pretext which the Western powers needed to bring the war to what they hoped would be its final phase. The battle begun in Western Slavonia in May could be ended only if the already strengthened Croatian and Bosnian armies could be helped decisively by what one journalist described as 'a fearsome display of military superiority' which only the Western powers could provide.[13]

The NATO tactic was not simply to push the Bosnian Serbs back from Sarajevo; in addition it was to fatally weaken them just as the Croatian and Bosnian armies were advancing. NATO aircraft flew a total of 3,400 sorties, attacking 56 targets with 350 aiming points within them:

> NATO took out the Serbs' most valuable cards, negating their most decisive advantages. NATO attacked the Serbs' ammunition and armaments manufacture and repair facilities—their most obvious advantage over the more numerous but less well armed Muslims.
>
> But, more important still, NATO punched out the Serbs' eyes and the nervous system of the Serb military machine. And one of the areas that they concentrated on was around Banja Luka, where there were strong air defences—the area where the most recent Croat and Muslim advances have since taken place.[14]

In public the Western powers urged the Bosnian and Croatian governments not to take advantage of the bombings. In practice, however, their advance could never have been so swift—moving through western Bosnia until they were within a short distance of the Bosnian Serb stronghold of Banja Luka—without the air strikes and without the tacit acceptance of the NATO powers that these could only benefit the enemies of the Bosnian Serbs.

The peace process

As the war in the former Yugoslavia took a more bloody turn, so the latest round of 'peace talks' got under way in Geneva. But in the short term the background to the talks saw the different powers in the former Yugoslavia fighting to gain and retain as much land as possible. The fighting has achieved what diplomacy was unable to do and the Bosnian Serbs were forced onto less and less land. 'The UN estimates that in the past month or so the proportion of land held by the rebels [Bosnian Serbs] has fallen from around 72 percent to around 55 percent,' wrote one journalist, Emma Daly, in mid-September.[15]

The formal peace plan—with 51 percent to the Muslim-Croat federation and 49 percent to a Bosnian Serb republic—represents a military *fait accompli*. The US sees this as vitally important. It has intervened to ensure that the Bosnian Serbs were sufficiently on the defensive that they would have to come to the negotiating table. The Bosnian government has had to rely heavily both on NATO air strikes and on the militarily superior Croatian army to take much of the land they have conquered in recent months. There were reports just before the ceasefire of the Bosnian Serbs regaining small areas of land, with the Bosnian government's army finding it difficult to hold its lines.

Those who hope that the settlement brokered by the US will result in a lasting peace are more than likely to be disappointed. Most importantly, the proposed deal itself merely reinforces the ethnic divisions exacerbated by the war. As one diplomat put it, 'If the peace sticks, what we've got is Greater Serbia, Greater Croatia and the Muslims as a self governing minority in Greater Croatia'.[16] The article in which this source was quoted goes on to say:

> We are now looking at ethnically pure states. There are virtually no Serbs left in Krajina in Croatia, although some 200,000 Serbs lived there until the Croat offensive. The enclave of Gorazde is the last puddle of Muslims left alive along the Drina Valley in eastern Bosnia, one of the great historical centres of Muslim population. Despite their multi-ethnic policies, there are few Croats and Serbs left in the Muslim dominated Bosnian government territories around Tuzla and Zenica in central Bosnia.
>
> 'Throughout the whole territory of Bosnia, ethnic cleansing is now nearly complete,' said Steve Curliss of the UN High Commission for Refugees after the fall of Zepa in July. Since Curliss said this, the UNHCR estimates that 417,000 people have left their homes in Bosnia and Croatia. These are the last tectonic shifts of ethnic cleansing.[17]

The ceasefire was from its very inception likely to cause still further ethnic cleansing. The day after it came into effect it was reported that 'some 40,000 Serb refugees were moving east last night towards Banja

Luka from the newly fallen towns. At the same time, thousands of the remaining Muslim residents of Serb held northern Bosnia had been forcibly expelled across the front lines by Serbs'.[18] There were an estimated 20,000 Muslims around Banja Luka until the ceasefire, all of whom were expected to be forcibly moved.

In any case, the deal is unlikely to work even in its own terms. There is still much dealing to be done, for example over Sarajevo, where Bosnian Croats want their own special sector of the city and the Serbs want it partitioned. The Bosnian government wants it intact as the capital city of Bosnia. Also much disputed are the narrow corridors of land which link the Muslim held Gorazde to other Muslim areas, and the Brcko corridor which links Serb areas in eastern Bosnia with Serb areas in the north round Banja Luka.

The plan is for a Peace Implemenenation Force to go into Bosnia to replace the discredited UN forces, many of whom will be withdrawn. These UN troops at present number around 28,000; the PIF will comprise 60,000 troops of whom one third will be US troops— and the total force is planned to be under US military command, although in the name of NATO. This represents an escalation of outside intervention, not a decline, with all the problems that entails. As one commentator spelt out:

> Intervention by outside forces has achieved precious little. Arguably, it has actually made the killing worse by prolonging the agony. Unarguably, it has done potentially irreparable damage to the Western alliance and to the standing of the United Nations. Peace has become a US show, implemented to raise the standing of President Bill Clinton in the eyes of his own electorate. US support of Croatia has upset the Russians and disturbed the Europeans.[19]

None of the parties directly concerned is particularly happy with the deal. The initial ceasefire came and went as all sides jockeyed for control of more land. The Bosnian government has taken advantage of its favoured position *vis-à-vis* the US government to hold out for more of its demands. For example, in the days before the original ceasefire date of 10 October 1995, the Bosnian government insisted on 'a tough NATO response' to violence in the Tuzla area as one of its conditions for the truce.[20]

The Croatian government will be happy with the Muslim-Croat federation which has control over the majority of Bosnia. But Croatia's expansionist aims have still not been satisfied. The army's success in the invasion of Krajina over the summer prompted calls for Croatia to take Eastern Slavonia, the last remaining Serb controlled area of Croatia. The area borders directly onto Serbia and there are fears that this would result in war between Croatia and Serbia. The UN inspired ceasefire there expires in November, and Croatia has said that it will take the region forcibly if 'peaceful reintegration' is not achieved by then. Retaking Eastern Slavonia was one of the main themes of the recent election campaign in Croatia.

The US ambassador to Croatia, Peter Galbraith, has desperately tried to broker a deal which allows Croatia to regain control of the area after a period of transition. However, Serbia wants this period to be five years rather than the 18 months favoured by Croatia, and, having witnessed the experience of the Krajina Serbs, they may be more than reluctant to come to any peaceful agreement.[21]

The Bosnian Serbs have found themselves forced onto the defensive in recent months, and have been in no position to go on the offensive in terms of territory or demands. Serbia has done nothing to help them, and President Milosevic has been instrumental in agreeing to the peace talks.

The international implications of the deal are no more encouraging. The US feels that it has done well in Bosnia. Peter Galbraith describes the Croat-Muslim federation as 'the cornerstone of our policy in the region'.[22] But there is unease among many of the other powers. Russia in particular has felt completely squeezed from an area where previously it had some influence. It also feels that NATO is playing too big a role in the area. Russian nationalists have urged Russian president Yeltsin to do more to help ethnic Serbs, and the Russian Duma has passed a resolution calling for the lifting of UN sanctions against Serbia and for imposing an embargo on Croatia. Hence the West's desire to pull Russia in more closely to the proposed peace, expressing a wish to use Russian troops in the Peace Implementation Force.

Britain has been dragged along in the wake of the NATO air strikes and US diplomacy, but it is disturbed by the diminished role of the UN, and its own lack of an independent voice in the maelstrom which is Bosnian politics. France under Chirac has taken a more aggressive stand than under the Mitterrand presidency. But both powers find themselves unhappy to be in the shadow of the US.

None of the powers, except possibly the US, are at all certain that the latest deal will succeed. But they see no real alternatives. The collapse of the former Yugoslavia has been aided and abetted by the various Western powers using incredibly cynical manoeuvres. Recognition of the independent states of Slovenia and Croatia by the most powerful EU state, Germany, at the end of 1991 helped to push the different republics to all out war and ensure that Bosnia would be carved up. This recognition came despite warnings that it was premature from, among others, the UN secretary general, Perez de Cuellar. Although Germany's decision was allegedly based on recognising the independence of any who wanted it, the German government refused to recognise another ex-Yugoslav republic, Macedonia, because fellow EU partner Greece was opposed to such a move.

Britain was persuaded to support the recognition of Croatia in return for generous German backing on the Maastricht Treaty opt out.[23] So the recognition came from a newly united Germany determined to make its diplomatic mark on the European scene, backed by a British Tory prime minister desperate to appease his own party and convince them that he was not making too many concessions to a federal Europe!

Since then the various Western powers have backed different warlords for their own particular ends. They have backed Milosevic and Serbia when they thought this was the chance of holding the former Yugoslavia together—under however nasty a nationalist regime. Now the major powers are prepared to back Croatian expansionism as a means of preserving 'peace' in the area, and all in the name of the underdog, the Bosnian Muslims. However, this means ignoring the atrocities committed by their current allies. So it is that an EU report about widespread Croat atrocities in Krajina is unlikely to be made public. As the *Guardian* says:

> Croatia is seen as a potential partner and is expected to join the Council of Europe next year. 'I think that at the end of the day, there's enough of an understanding with Croatia to let sleeping dogs lie,' a European diplomat said. 'It does leave a bad taste in people's mouths but if one of the prices of a peaceful settlement will be closer relations between the EU, Croatia and the others, then so be it'.[24]

The UN has taken a similar double standard approach. A recent statement on atrocities in Krajina 'was mild, saying only that the UN was "seriously concerned" for ethnic Serbs left in Krajina. A diplomatic source had an explanation for the tone: "Croatia is far too important geo-politically at the moment for the UN to make a fuss".'[25]

These statements simply sum up the complete cynicism with which the West has intervened. It has brought the region no nearer to real peace, and has been prepared to tolerate atrocities as long as they fit in with Western interests. The result of Western intervention has meant that things have become much worse. The latest peace deal presents no answer to those in the region who want a multi-ethnic and peaceful solution.

The biggest bully in the Balkans

The increasingly dominant and most ruthless player in the whole region is the US government. The latest stage of the war has been engineered and directed by and in its interests. The US ambassador to Croatia, Peter Galbraith—son of the establishment liberal J K Galbraith—has played an absolutely central role in getting the Croatian and Bosnian governments together, persuading them into military alliance and then federation, ensuring that the Western powers are prepared to back this federation while keeping Russia on board in the whole peace process. Galbraith has acquiesced to and indeed encouraged the invasion of Krajina. His reference in the Croatian airline's magazine to the Krajina Serbs as 'so called local Serbs', despite their having lived in the area for hundreds of years, gives some feel of the US determination to ride roughshod over reality in order to get their way, regardless of the human cost. According to the *Washington Post*:

> US officials, concerned with providing a counterweight to Serbia, helped Croatia avoid sanctions in 1993. Ambassador Peter Galbraith led the US effort to stop the Muslim-Croat war and helped hammer out a new mandate for the UN peacekeeping force in Croatia earlier this year. As part of the mandate, the UN Security Council passed a resolution recognising Croatia's territorial integrity. Croatia used that…resolution as a legal justification for launching Operation Storm.[26]

It is clear that the present US envoy who has brokered the peace, Richard Holbrooke, has only been able to do so because the ground has been laid by the brutal escalation of the war in recent months. In short, the Bosnian Serb leaders have been forced to the negotiating table very largely by US efforts aimed at strengthening their opponents and putting pressure on their allies. So while Milosevic put pressure on the Bosnian Serbs up to two years ago, limiting their supplies from Serbia, at the same time:

Mr Galbraith cracked Muslim and Croat heads together and told them they would never recover territory lost to the Serbs in Croatia and Bosnia unless they stopped fighting each other and formed a common front...with Mr Galbraith's encouragement, Croatia built up a well trained and well equipped army capable of taking on the Serbs.[27]

The US has been busy elsewhere in the region. It again was responsible for the deal in September this year between Greece and the former Yugoslav republic of Macedonia. The region has been a source of anxiety and instability since the break up of Yugoslavia, when Greece, backed by Serbia, refused to recognise any state taking the name of Macedonia. The new deal allows Greece to recognise the republic, but under a different name. The US, which has 1,000 of its troops stationed on Macedonia's border with Serbia, is also linking the Bosnian peace deal with recognition.

The US tactic is to deploy a combination of bribery and brute force which will make all the players accept the existing division of land in Bosnia which corresponds relatively closely to the peace plan. US military superiority will do the rest. They fear what they call a 'Berlin-style solution' in Bosnia where different segments are policed by their respective international supporters—for example, Russia in Bosnian Serb territories. To this end, they are willing to pull Russia onto their side—even talking about creating a NATO peacekeeping body which consists of the 16 NATO countries plus Russia. Peace through strength seems to be the US slogan. It and its allies want:

> ...the dispatch of a powerful force early on to deter last minute grabs for extra land by one side or other... Once this force is in place, the alliance hopes it can persuade the better armed belligerents to reduce their own forces. Otherwise, Washington would be happy to see the less well equipped Muslim army 'professionalised and retrained'.[28]

The *Financial Times* reported recently that Richard Holbrooke 'does not see any contradiction...in mediating the peace while...training, and even re-equipping, the Bosnian army.' At the same time, he is trying to get the Muslim fundamentalist volunteers inside the Bosnian army to leave the country.[29]

Whether the US and its allies will be able to enforce the deal remains an open question. But there is no doubt that the misery, chaos and divisions which at present exist in former Yugoslavia will not be helped by such intervention. Rather, it is likely to strengthen many of the nastier elements in each respective ethnic group. Certainly the US has had no qualms about backing policies and methods which are a very long way from the peace and democracy which it publicly professes.

Should the left take sides?

The demand to take the side of Bosnia in this dispute has been widespread on the left. But any serious evaluation of the various Bosnian, Croatian and Serbian authorities reveals similar features: politicians and party bosses who have been prepared to use nationalist rhetoric in order to bolster their support and to strengthen their own and their supporters' positions; relatively small if extremely unpleasant groups of brutal nationalists and ethnic cleansers who have used rape, torture and killing to get their way and who have often been at least covertly sanctioned by their 'respectable' political leaders; and the mass of ordinary people who have lived in some sort of peaceful coexistence with members of other ethnic groups for decades, and who now face the choice of fleeing for their lives, leaving homes and possessions behind, or of seeing their erstwhile neighbours and friends having to flee.

These are the real victims of this war, and theirs is a suffering of which the Western rulers know little and care even less. Given this, it is astonishing how even now there are individual stories of decency and humanity. But any chance of nurturing that decency is rapidly and surely being squeezed out in the name of revenge, or 'sticking with one's own', or having to back one particular ethnic group.

Those media commentators who only highlight the atrocities of one group and ignore those of the others are simply helping to shore up the nationalism and ethnic hatred. Misha Glenny begins one of the chapters of his book *The Fall of Yugoslavia* with three separate personal descriptions from a Croat refugee in Zagreb, a Muslim refugee in Sarajevo and a Serb refugee in Belgrade. All are completely horrific and all could apply to any of the ethnic groups.[30] Glenny is extremely critical of the nationalists on all sides, and has a strong distaste for the Serb nationalists, but this does not cloud his judgement about the facts. Indeed, he argues repeatedly that the Serbs are systematically treated unfairly in the Western media.

He points out, for example, that despite the idea that Serbia is the main aggressor in the region, Croatia too should have had UN sanctions imposed on it in 1992, since it was in violation of a UN resolution. Instead it received only a slap on the wrist, enabling its economy to perform much better than Serbia's.[31] He also points out that 'the majority of UNPROFOR members and aid workers who have died during this conflict have been the victims of Muslim units and, to a lesser extent, Croat ones'.[32] The reason they have got away with this, says Glenny, is that they have won the propaganda war in the Western media. They have constantly used this sympathy to launch attacks which are barely reported; when Serbian nationalists have retaliated—often in a brutal fashion— this is condemned by the West without the original attack being mentioned.[33] The same is true when it comes to questions of killings, rapes and other atrocities, when much more space in Western newspapers is devoted to the crimes of the Bosnian Serbs than to any other. But what of the various regimes themselves?

Serbia

It is commonplace on the left to regard the Serbian state as by far the most dictatorial of the three players in the war. Indeed, some even regard it as fascist. The regime is unpleasant, right wing and nationalistic—although this does not distinguish it in qualitative terms from that of Tudjman in Croatia. But it is far from being a fascist regime, where the working class movement has been totally crushed. Its leader, Slobodan Milosevic, is a nasty, right wing, careerist politician who has used nationalism and war in order to strengthen his position and to isolate liberal or left wing opponents. But the nationalism of Milosevic is much more opportunist than it is deeply ideological. In the late 1980s he managed to deflect political and industrial protest which was resulting from the economic crisis in the former Yugoslavia by playing the nationalist card. When the crisis caused by trying to hold the confederation together led to moves for independence from the various republics, Milosevic greatly exacerbated fears that Serbs within Croatia and Bosnia were under the most dire threat and so helped to fuel further national antagonisms. However, he also took a pragmatic view towards the independence of the republics. By January 1991:

> Milosevic had already decided; if Yugoslavia could not be salvaged and centralised, then the Croats, like the Slovenes, would be allowed to go. But they would not be allowed to take with them those parts of their republic that Milosevic's men considered Serb territory.[34]

It was to this end that he held a meeting with Tudjman before war broke out where the two men agreed secretly to partition Bosnia between them, and after which Tudjman triumphantly claimed that he had doubled the size of Croatia.[35] Now, four years later, many people believe that there has been a further understanding between the two men, as a result of which Milosevic has 'turned a deaf ear to calls for help' from the Krajina and Bosnian Serbs.[36] Before the Croatian invasion of Krajina, tanks, artillery and top officers controlled by the Krajina Serb military were withdrawn, leaving the population defenceless. Whether this was with the collusion of Milosevic or the Yugoslav army, the JNA, is not known. But certainly Milosevic has done little in recent months to help the Serb refugees and has been extremely compliant with Western demands over the peace process.

However, Milosevic may be pushed to the limit by the refusal of Croatia and Bosnia to accept the agreed parameters of the peace plan, with the Croatian army still threatening invasion of Eastern Slavonia as this journal went to press, while both Bosnian and Croatian armies are pushing for further territories up to and including the Serb stronghold and now teeming refugee centre of Banja Luka. 'The dispatch [to Banja Luka] from Belgrade of the warlord Zeljko "Arkan" Raznjatovic and his ferocious Tigers, suggests that...Milosevic finally has drawn a line in the sand around Bosnia's second city'.[37] Whether this turns out to be the case, support for the Bosnian Serb leadership now comes much more from the far right and the Orthodox church patriarchy than from Milosevic and his supporters. The church has described the president as a 'godless Communist', and last year Milosevic vetoed a church sponsored bill to restrict abortion.[38]

The state over which Milosevic presides is by no means the monolithic Serb nationalist entity that is often portrayed as being. As the *Washington Post* puts it:

Compared to Croatia, Milosevic's Serbia, with an estimated 6.4 million Serbs, 1.7 million Albanians, 345,000 Hungarians, 235,000 Muslims and 130,000 Croats, is a multi-ethnic state. According to the 1991 census, only 65 percent of Serbia's 9.8 million population is Serb.[39]

Milosevic senses that people in Serbia are war weary, and that they want sanctions against them to be lifted. The fall in the level of gross domestic product per head among the Serbian population has been dramatic since the war began. This has had serious effects on living standards, with many people forced to sell smuggled goods on the streets of Belgrade to make any sort of living.[40] There are severe food, fuel and medicine shortages, and a 50 percent unemployment rate.[41]

But the impact of the huge number of refugees flooding into Serbia itself, plus the sense that the Serbs are getting less and less out of the peace deal and that they are constantly reviled in the Western media, plus the fact that economic sanctions are bringing real hardship to millions of people, all mean that Milosevic can strengthen his support.

Croatia

Croatia today enjoys favoured status with both the US and the EU. It is on the fast track to membership of the EU, which means that it receives military, financial and other material help from the Western powers. Its leader, the former Communist boss Franjo Tudjman, is determined to establish a dominant Croatia in the region at the expense of the Serbian state's influence, but also no doubt at the cost of his current allies, the Bosnian Muslims. Tudjman, egged on by Croatian emigrés who returned at the time of independence four years ago, has been willing to use the trappings of the pro-Nazi wartime Ustashe regime which spent four years battling against the Partisans in the very same areas in which fighting now takes place. In particular, the chequered flag is enough to strike terror into the hearts of many Serbs, who suffered terrible repression at the hands of the Ustashe during the Second World War.

This does not seem to cause Tudjman much disquiet. He is known for his view that the Holocaust was much exaggerated, and for his statement, 'Thank god my wife is not a Jew or a Serb'.[42] The well known Nazi-hunter Simon Wiesenthal has said that Croatia's 1,200 Jews are living in fear.[43] A recent video issued in Zagreb, entitled *Five Years of Croatian Freedom*, portrays him in a white uniform with huge epaulettes reviewing military hardware from the back of a jeep. The video describes Tudjman as the 'igniter of the drowsing spirit of the fatherland'.[44]

The state over which Tudjman presides is now the most 'ethnically clean' state in the former Yugoslavia. It is estimated that over 90 percent of its population are now Croats, compared with 78 percent in 1991.[45] Not only have the vast majority of the country's Serbs now left but there are also signs that Croatia is putting up barriers to Muslim refugees, despite its alliance with the Bosnian government. Muslims attempting to escape Bosnian Serb areas have been refused entry into

Croatia and so have been trapped on the Bosnian side of the border. Those forced out of areas such as Banja Luka by the Bosnian Serbs have received little help from Croatia. A report in late August said:

> Non-Serbs in Banja Luka and other parts of north western Bosnia have been subjected to a renewed campaign of terror in recent days as Serb refugees from Krajina have been physically dislodged from their homes. Roman Catholic Croats who are victims of this campaign have been allowed into Croatia, but the Zagreb authorities are much less keen to accept Muslims.[46]

Recently Tudjman told the French paper *Le Figaro* that Croatia would gladly assume the burden of 'civilising the Muslims' after the war, and that Tito's greatest mistake was to grant the Muslims national rights in the 1960s.[47]

The Croatian state has very limited opposition within it. The editor of one of the country's newspapers, *Globus*, was ousted after the invasion of Krajina. The editor claimed that the reason for this was the paper's 'lack of sufficient patriotism' in covering Operation Storm.[48] It is clearly hard for dissenting voices to be heard in the atmosphere of jingoism that has existed in Croatia in recent months. The state dominates the media. Although there are opposition parties, 'for the time being at least they are all singing the same tune. The Social Liberals' leader, Drazen Budisa, declared it was not the time to criticise, but a "time to rejoice".'[49]

Yet this militaristic and nationalistic state—described by an opposition political commentator as a modern Sparta—is one which has been feted and aided by the West and which is being groomed for membership of the EU. The IMF and World Bank, as well as the EU, are willing to lend Croatia money. And funds have already been flowing into the coffers of Croatia's reserves from rich returning emigrés. Last May the country's national bank reported $1.6 billion foreign reserves, compared with $600 million in 1993.[50] The fact that Croatia has avoided Western sanctions and has been able to quite openly flout the arms embargo—creaming off an estimated 20 to 30 percent of weapons designed for the Bosnian government—has widened the gap between it and its rival Serbia:

> In 1991 Serbia had a per capita gross domestic product of $2,330, about the same as Croatia. In 1993...that number sank in Serbia to $1,225. Croatia's jumped to $3,048 in 1993 and $3,132 in 1994.[51]

Even so, unemployment is rising and military spending this year is estimated to run at 41 percent of government expenditure.[52] Tudjman called an election a year early to improve the majority of the ruling HDZ (Croatian Democratic Union), making it more dominant in parliament. Just to try and make sure, Tudjman pushed through a new law which allows Croats abroad—mainly in Bosnia—to vote. At the same time, the electoral status of Croatian Serbs has been reduced, since only three seats for national minorities are guaranteed in the parliament, as opposed to the previous 13.[53] Even US observers have been appalled at the lack of democracy in Croatia. 'Reserving almost 10 percent of all seats to people living permanently outside of a state is unprecedented,' according to Washington's National Democratic Institute's report on the election.[54] In the event, Tudjman's HDZ did not get the required two thirds majority to make constitutional changes, thus showing that there is less support for Tudjman than has been thought.

Bosnia

The Bosnian state is seen as the underdog by many in the West, because it seems sandwiched between two aggressive warring powers. Yet there are crucial peculiarities in the make up of Bosnia which helps to explain some of its recent history. Before the war most people living in the region referred to themselves simply as Bosnians rather than adding Serb, Croat or Muslim.[55]

The multi-ethnic make up of Bosnia meant that any attempt at independence would create major problems. As Misha Glenny says:

> Bosnia's national mix ensures that it cannot be divided without war. At the same time, Bosnia has never existed, since the medieval kingdom, as an independent state... Bosnia has always survived by dint of a protective shield provided either by a Yugoslav state or the Austrian or Ottoman empires.[56]

The Bosnian Muslims found the choice of either staying in a much reduced Yugoslavia or being partitioned between Serbia and Croatia profoundly unattractive. They were therefore caught between a rock and a hard place when the former Yugoslavia broke up.

However, the idea that the Bosnian government is an innocent victim of aggression is impossible to sustain. In fact, the Bosnian president, Alia Izetbegovic, was the first to organise a political party for the

Muslims along nationalist lines when the SDA was formed in 1990. It was described at the time as 'a political alliance of Yugoslav citizens belonging to Muslim cultural and historical traditions'.[57] The SDA campaigned for the break up of the former Yugoslavia and for recognition of all six Yugoslav republics, saying that Bosnia could not remain in a Serb dominated federation.[58]

Various Muslim paramilitary organisations were formed in Bosnia once the war started, such as the Patriotic League and the Green Berets, who wore the official Bosnian coat of arms. Misha Glenny wrote of the Green Berets in 1992 that they 'have recruited from the criminal classes and the lumpenproletariat and they have already injected their own brand of corruption into Sarajevo's enforced war economy'.[59]

The Muslims have suffered and continue to suffer terrible atrocities. But they too have been guilty of ethnic cleansing, killing and rape.[60] There is evidence that the state run from Sarajevo is decreasingly multi-ethnic. Bosnian television is run by an SDA member who is fervently in favour of a Muslim identity for Bosnia. Only Muslims in the SDA are able to rise high in the administration, media, army or business.[61] The war's development has meant an influx into the towns of refugees from rural areas, who have very different values from many of the liberal ideals which dominated Sarajevo, and the return of exiles who have come back to fight for Bosnia and who reflect strong feelings of nationalism and ethnic identity.[62]

In recent months the Bosnian government and its supporters have become increasingly vocal and aggressive in their demands. The Bosnian government has long understood that it can get away with a great deal because of US backing and the way in which the Western governments see the Bosnian Muslims as innocent victims: 'Throughout the war they have used this perception to undertake offensive actions and then portray themselves as victims'.[63] But since the latest phase of the war brought the military alliance with Croatia, they have been even more confident.

Most recently, Bosnian government forces have been involved in continuing fighting in north west Bosnia, despite the ceasefire. Their aim is clearly to control the whole area up to and including Banja Luka. The army is determined to press the advantage it gained with the help of the stronger Croatian army and the NATO air strikes. One of its generals was quoted as saying around the time of the ceasefire, 'Of course, we will respect the orders of our political leadership if they tell us to stop, but if we give up on going home, our people will never accept it'.[64] But some of the area being fought over is land which was never 'home' to the Bosnian Muslims: 'Mrkonjic Grad, which fell [in October] was 77 percent Serb; Petrovac, Drvar and Grahovo, which fell to the Croats earlier on, were more than 95 percent Serb'.[65]

Recently the Bosnian vice-president demanded more than the 51 percent of territory offered to the Muslim-Croatian federation under the peace plan, arguing that the Bosnian Serbs inside the Serb controlled areas now amounted to only 400,000 people—or 11 percent of the pre-war population, compared to the 32 percent they had comprised before the war.[66]

These attitudes reflect the harder line taken by Bosnian leaders in recent months and mark a move away from multi-ethnicity and towards the Bosnian government trying to carve out a bigger share of territory and influence. The government crisis which arose temporarily when the prime minister, Haris Silajdzic, tried (unsuccessfully) to resign in the summer seemed to be caused by his resistance to this hard line, which is epitomised by his rival, the Bosnian foreign minister, Mohamed Sacirbey. Sacirbey is a Wall Street lawyer who was born in Sarajevo but has lived most of his life in the US. This former vice-president of the merchant bank Security Pacific has made it his mission, first as Bosnian ambassador to the UN and then as foreign minister, to portray Bosnia as the underdog while at the same time pulling the US into the war on its side. 'He aims to "Americanise" the Bosnian conflict, drawing the US into a full scale war against the Serbs'.[67] He has clearly been successful.

The Bosnian government quite rightly fears the expansionist intent of Croatia, but government leaders have opened the door to a Greater Croatia, in which eventually they too will prove the losers.

Conclusion

The various states involved in the conflict are all, to one degree or another, nationalistic and increasingly ethnically based. Socialists can find nothing to support in these regimes, and those who make the mistake of backing one side are increasingly finding themselves faced with contradictions as the supposedly multi-ethnic states become more 'cleansed' and more narrowly based. They also miss out on a range of opposition among the populations of each state who have reacted against being sold the empty promise of national glory and military success.

One of the most hideous aspects of war is the way in which governments, media and top military tend to act and speak on the assumption that 'their' population is totally behind them, and that the 'enemy' population is equally behind its own rulers. The reality is usually very different. Of course it is true that there are times when jingoism and pro-war sentiments prevail among the mass of people, but for the majority of the time among the majority of people there is no glorification of war.

It is easy to understand why this should be when we look at the situation in the former Yugoslavia. War there has involved the displacement of an estimated two million people and death, rape, torture and other forms of barbarism inflicted on many thousands. Even for those who have escaped these horrors, day to day life for workers has been hard. And the threat of war is ever present.

But there has been opposition to the war. Indeed, it can be argued that the war itself started as an attempt to dampen class struggle directed at the country's rulers and to turn workers against other workers and peasants of a different ethnic background. As the war began in March 1991 tens of thousands of students and workers marched in Belgrade against repression and for democracy; up to half a million occupied the city centre. After war spread to Bosnia in 1992 the anti-war movement in Belgrade organised a demonstration and a 100,000 strong concert against the war. In 1993 in the Serbian capital 1,500 people demonstrated on the first anniversary of the siege of Sarajevo.[68]

War weariness has also been evident in Croatia, where the Anti-War Campaign of Croatia was formed in 1991, and where there have been strikes including a half hour general strike against lower living standards in 1993. There has also been a rash of short strikes recently to recover unpaid wages.[69]

None of these adds up to a major campaign against the war, but that is hardly surprising given the terrible suffering in recent years, and the destruction of lives and livelihoods. Equally, it is no wonder that nationalist and right wing ideas come to dominate among a wider layer of the population. But these ideas are not all powerful. As grievances begin to build up, so many ordinary workers and peasants question the role of their leaders and the nationalist politics on which they are based. It is then that there is the possibility of alternative ideas coming to the fore, then that people begin to look to their interests as similar to those of other workers even across the ethnic divides. A recent *Assignment* television programme, introduced by the

journalist Allan Little, showed one Krajina Serb who had been displaced to Serbia sending a video message to two middle aged Croats,
themselves ethnically cleansed from Banja Luka, who were trying to
take over his house. The message said that they should not feel guilty,
because they were just victims—as were all ordinary Serbs, Croats
and Muslims—of the nationalist rulers, and now they were having to
pay the bill.[70] It was a powerful testimony to ordinary people's ability
to see through the nationalist propaganda of their rulers.

Perhaps this is not a typical sentiment, but the horrors of the former
Yugoslavia are drawing people to thinking about alternatives. Imagine the buffeting, physical and ideological, which has been the lot of
the Krajina Serbs. They believed much of the nationalist rhetoric
from their own leaders and the Serbian leaders. Now they are homeless, jobless, split up from their families, forced to live in the isolated
province of Kosovo. This does not mean that all or most of them will
draw socialist or left wing conclusions—but it does mean that the old
certainties have broken down. For example, one Krajina Serb from
Knin, now living in a Belgrade tower block, was quoted as saying, 'I
don't want to throw any Croats out of their homes, but I would throw
Milosevic out of his house for what he has done to us'.[71]

In the big cities of Belgrade and Zagreb there is opposition to the
rulers from a wide spectrum of people. But the nature of war in its
early and successful phase is that it silences much opposition. That can
begin to change as circumstances change, and it is then that we can
hold out hope for an alternative, class based solution to the problems
of the region. We know already that, despite the warmongering, most
people do not want war. For example, there are many recent reports
of Bosnian Serbs of call up age moving to Serbia to avoid the draft. Up
to 60,000 have fled to Montenegro.

But the nationalist leaders, the UN, NATO and the Western powers
have all acted to ensure that war has endured. As one commentator
put it:

> The UN has failed. NATO, the European Union and even the Red
> Cross have failed. Diplomacy, mediation, peacekeeping, humanitar-
> ianism and the New World Order have all failed. Brute force has
> succeeded.[72]

It need not be that way. But the alternative lies in the ordinary people
who are suffering so much in this war understanding that their interests
do not lie in backing their own ruling classes along national lines, but

in fighting for a democratic, multi-ethnic society—which means fighting their own ruling classes, the cynical interventions of the Western powers, and all those (such as the far right and religious organisations) who want to divide them on ethnic or national lines. The Russian revolutionary Leon Trotsky was a journalist in the Balkans before the First World War, when, as now, war tore the area to pieces. In 1910 he wrote:

> State unity of the Balkan peninsula can be achieved in two ways: either from above, by expanding one Balkan state, whichever proves strongest, at the expense of the weaker ones—this is the road of wars of extermination and oppression of weak nations, a road that consolidates monarchism and militarism; or from below, through the peoples themselves coming together—this is the road of revolution, the road that means overthrowing the Balkan dynasties and unfurling the banner of a Balkan federal republic.[73]

These are the options facing workers and peasants in the area. At present the first road is being followed, with disastrous consequences. The only way to win democracy and multi-ethnicity is for socialists to reject the national solutions and to argue that only the second road provides any real solution to the problems that the Balkan people face.

Notes

1   'Croatia's Blitzkrieg', *Economist*, 12 August 1995.

2   S Crawshaw, 'East Slavonia Braces For The Final Battle', *Independent*, 30 September 1995.

3   See M Glenny, *The Fall of Yugoslavia* (second edition, London, 1993), p86, where he describes how left wingers he spoke to in London seemed to have a totally uncritical view of Croatian nationalism.

4   *Independent*, 7 August 1995.

5   M Foot, 'New Hope In The Balkans', *Tribune*, 25 August 1995.

6   'Momentum Shifts In Balkan War', *Washington Post*, 22 August 1995.

7   'UN Says Croats Putting Krajina To Torch', *Financial Times*, 22 August 1995.

8   'The Flight Of The Krajina Serbs', *Economist*, 12 August 1995.

9   'UN Reports Looting In Ex-Serb Area', *Washington Post*, 22 August 1995.

10   R Fisk, quoted in 'Croats Burn And Kill With A Vengeance', *Independent*, 4 September 1995.

11   See R Fisk, 'Croats Slaughter Elderly By The Dozen', *Independent*, 10 September 1995, and 'Face To Face With Ethnic Cleansers', *Independent*, 14 September 1995.

12   'In Balkans, Imbalance Of Power', *USA Today*, 14 August 1995.

13   See T Barber, 'Brute Force Reshapes Balkans', *Independent on Sunday*, 17 September 1995.

14   C Bellamy, 'How NATO Paralysed Serb Command', *Independent on Sunday*, 17 September 1995.

15   E Daly, 'Double Vision Blurs Peace Map', *Independent on Sunday*, 17 September 1995.

16   Quoted in C Eagar, 'Future Bosnia Shot To Pieces', *Observer*, 8 October 1995.

17   Ibid.

18   'Bosnia Ceasefire Is Finally Agreed By All Sides', *Independent*, 12 October 1995.

19   A Hamilton, 'Cost Of A Bosnian Peace Made In America May Be Too High A Price To Pay', *Observer*, 8 October 1995.

20   'Bosnia Ceasefire Plan Fails At Last Minute', *Financial Times*, 10 October 1995.

21   'Serbs And Croats Strike East Slavonia Deal', *Independent*, 4 October 1995.

22   'US Optimism Over Ceasefire Deal In Bosnia', *Independent*, 30 September 1995.

23   See M Glenny, *The Fall of Yugoslavia*, op cit, p192.

24   J Borger, 'EU Report Accuses Croatia Of Atrocities Against Rebel Serbs', *Guardian*, 30 September 1995.

25   C Eagar, 'Future Bosnia Shot To Pieces', op cit.

26   'Momentum Shifts In Balkan War', *Washington Post*, 22 August 1995.

27   T Barber, op cit.

28   R Cornwell, 'US Woos Russia For Peace Force', *Independent*, 7 October 1995.

29   Q Peel, 'US Sets Out To Give Peace Its Best Shot', *Financial Times*, 30 October 1995.

30   See M Glenny, op cit, pp181-182.

31   Ibid, p211.

32   Ibid, pp201-202.

33   See ibid for example, p221.

34   L Silber and A Little, *The Death of Yugoslavia* (London 1995), p127.

35   Ibid, p143.
36   See for example E Mortimer, 'Slicing Up The Bosnian Cake', *Financial Times*, 8 August 1995.
37   M Tanner, 'A Farewell To Arms—But For How Long?', *Independent on Sunday*, 15 October 1995.
38   P Hockenos, 'Letter From Belgrade', *New Statesman and Society*, 14 July 1995.
39   *Washington Post*, 22 August 1995.
40   Ibid.
41   See S Sagall, 'Reluctant Soldiers', *Socialist Review*, September 1995.
42   See L Silber and A Little, op cit, p92.
43   S Masterman, 'Poll Blow For "Corrupt" Croat Chief', *Evening Standard*, 31 October 1995.
44   J Borger, 'Victorious Croatia Closes Doors To Ethnic Minorities', *Guardian*, 21 August 1995.
45   'Momentum Shifts In Balkan War', *Washington Post*, op cit.
46   'UN Says Croats Putting Krajina To Torch', *Financial Times*, 22 August 1995.
47   'Heading Home', *New Statesman and Society*, 13 October 1995.
48   *Washington Post*, 22 August 1995.
49   J Borger, op cit.
50   *Washington Post*, 22 August 1995.
51   Ibid.
52   See S Sagall, op cit.
53   L Silber, 'Tudjman Expects Poll Win', *Financial Times*, 30 October 1995.
54   T Barber 'Croat Army Poised To Grab East Slavonia', *Independent*, 17 October 1995.
55   M Glenny, op cit, p143.
56   Ibid, p144.
57   L Silber and A Little, op cit, p228.
58   Ibid, p238.
59   M Glenny, op cit, p161.
60   See for example ibid, pp161, 218, 221.
61   'The Coffee Cup State', *Economist*, 26 August 1995.
62   See for example L Bryant, 'Heading Home', *New Statesman and Society*, 13 October 1995.
63   M Glenny, op cit, p201.
64   L Bryant, op cit.
65   M Tanner, op cit.
66   T Barber, 'Land Claim Upsets Peace Plan', *Independent*, 18 October 1995.
67   B Webb and S Guirao, 'From Wall Street To Sarajevo', *New Statesman and Society*, 28 July 1995.
68   S Sagall, op cit.
69   Ibid.
70   *Assignment*, BBC2, 21 October 1995.
71   P Morgan, 'Letter From Belgrade', *New Statesman*, 27 October 1995.
72   E Mortimer, 'Slicing Up The Bosnian Cake', *Financial Times*, 8 August 1995.
73   L Trotsky, *The Balkan Wars 1912-13* (New York, 1980).

Chapter 16

No 'liberation' in Bosnia

Chris Harman

Socialist Review's articles on Bosnia have met with hostility from many sections of the left. How can you refuse, they say, to support the national liberation struggle of 'multi-ethnic' Bosnia against the Serbs?

Such arguments reveal the degree of confusion that exists on much of the left. What has been tearing Bosnia apart for the last three years has been a three sided struggle between rival nationalisms.

The sociologist Laslo Skelj has traced the rebirth of nationalism to the reaction of Yugoslavia's rulers to the student revolt which shook the regime in 1968. In a desperate attempt to fragment opposition to themselves, they encouraged nationalism among each ethnic group, with the central regime playing one nationalism off against another, while still imprisoning dissidents who took this nationalism too far.

The economic crisis of the late 1980s, a huge strike wave and the collapse of the other Eastern European regimes, threw all the rulers into panic. In each republic they set out to divert developing class bitterness into a frenzy of nationalist agitation which left themselves secure.

Milosevic of Serbia pioneered this strategy, but Slovenian, Croatian, Macedonian and Bosnian Muslim leaders were soon following suit.

The nationalism played a reactionary role everywhere. But it was particularly pernicious in regions where the different nationalities lived alongside each other. In the border regions of Croatia and in Bosnia the outcome was civil war.

Ethnically based states can only ever be formed in areas of mixed populations if one group imposes its supremacy on others. The horrific logic of this is inter-communal civil war and ethnic cleansing—the use of terror to drive members of rival groups from captured areas so as to

First published November 1995

secure them permanently. Atrocity then breeds counter-atrocity as the front line shifts and each side forces out potential opponents.

In such situations the answer is not to back one lot of nationalists against their rivals, one sort of ethnic cleansing against the other. It is to stand for the unity of workers and peasants against the nationalist demagogues on both sides.

It is not as if the Bosnian Muslims are an historically oppressed national group deserving special support. Under the Ottoman Empire for centuries the ruling elite in the province was Muslim, not Serb. During the Second World War the Muslim upper classes collaborated with the Croat fascist Ustashe to oppress the Serbs, carting hundreds of thousands off to concentration camps. The Tito regime persecuted Muslim dissidents no more than any others, ensuring that every time a Muslim was imprisoned so was a Serb and a Croat. Only during the brief period between the two world wars were Muslims in any sense the underdogs in the Yugoslav kingdom.

Izetbegovic's Muslim SDA sought to build itself with the collapse of Yugoslavia, as much as Karadzic's Serb SDS and the Bosnian wing of Tudjman's HDZ. Each saw its aim as being to advance the aims of one nationality at the expense of others.

So, as former BBC World Service correspondent Misha Glenny tells, where the SDA took control of local councils it sacked many Serbs and Croats from their jobs. When Izetbegovic built a paramilitary formation, the Green Berets, again it was recruited entirely from Muslims.

The only difference between Izetbegovic and the rival nationalist leaders was that he was in a weaker position, since Muslims amounted to less than half of Bosnia's population and could not look to powerful external allies in the same way as the Bosnian Croat and Bosnian Serb nationalists.

Yet Izetbegovic made clear that he was prepared to go to war for a Bosnian republic in which his party would be the dominant force. 'I would sacrifice peace for a sovereign Bosnia-Hercegovina,' he told parliament in February 1991, and proclaimed national independence the following year after a referendum which the overwhelming majority of Serbs had boycotted.

The result was that the Serb nationalists and Milosevic's government in Serbia proper found it easy to persuade most Bosnian Serbs to join them in a nationalist attempt to partition Bosnia. Just as Muslim nationalism demanded the setting up of Bosnia as a Muslim led state, so Serbian nationalism demanded the breakaway of a majority Serb state.

But this was only achievable by using terror to drive out Muslim and Croat populations from wide areas of the country. Soon the Croats were effectively doing the same in the Mostar-Vitez area, even while retaining seats in Tudjman's government—and Muslim troops were retaliating in kind.

What is true is that Serbia enjoyed military superiority for the first two years of the war, and so most ethnic cleansing was by the Serb forces. Tudjman's weak position forced him to talk of a 'multi-ethnic' Bosnia. This was at the same time as his party forced members of other ethnic groups from key civil service jobs and tolerated the Green Berets and other paramilitaries driving Serbs from their homes.

The US-NATO bombing of Serb positions and the arming of the Croats—and to a lesser extent the Muslims—by the US has now changed the situation. It is the Muslim and, especially, the Croat armies which are surging forward. The result has been the 'cleansing' of hundreds of thousands of Serbs from the towns of the Croatian Krajina and north eastern Bosnia, which the Western media virtually ignore while giving enormous publicity to atrocities by Serb troops.

Yet sections of the left treat the Croat and Bosnian armies as if they were 'liberators'. In fact Tudjman, whose army has received most of the US arms and training, is clearly playing a double game—hoping both to seize Eastern Slavonia from Serbia (with still more ethnic cleansing) and to establish his own dominance over a rump Muslim state in the US backed Muslim-Croat federation. Meanwhile, Izetbegovic is upsetting those Croat and Serb figures in Sarajevo and Tuzla who once believed his talk of a 'multi-ethnic Bosnia'.

Chapter 17

Electoral cleansing

Sabby Sagall

Western rulers and NATO commanders have greeted the Bosnian elections with a fanfare of complacent rhetoric. The elections were supposed to end four years of bloody civil war, to preserve Bosnia's territorial integrity and to begin to reverse the ethnic cleansing of two million people (out of a pre-war population of 4.4 million of whom 44 percent were Muslim, 31 percent Serb and 17 percent Croat). Under the US-brokered Dayton agreement which ended the war last November, refugees displaced from their land and homes were to be allowed to return.

There were to be no less than seven different elections: for the three person joint presidency of the whole country, for the president of the Serb republic, a national parliament, separate assemblies in the Bosnian Serb republic and the Muslim-Croatian federation, 'cantons' in the Muslim-Croatian federation and, finally, local municipal elections. Votes were allocated to territory and not ethnic group (51 percent of the country was allocated according to the Muslim-Croatian federation and 49 percent to the Bosnian Serb republic). And people could register to vote in the areas where they lived before the outbreak of hostilities in April 1992. A NATO force of 60,000, including 20,000 US troops, was dispatched to police the elections and to facilitate repatriation.

The US government argued that Bosnians, if given a choice, would vote for candidates standing for reconstruction rather than war. They also seemed to believe that the conditions for free elections could be created: freedom of expression, assembly and movement, free and equal access to the media by all shades of opinion and open debate.

What has been achieved? The fighting has stopped (for now). There has been an exchange of prisoners and territory. NATO troops removed mines and barricades from the military frontline, allowing anyone, in theory, to come and go at will.

First published October 1996

But the balance sheet leans heavily on the debit side. War criminals, meant to be arrested, have roamed freely over the country. The boundary line became in many cases too dangerous to cross. An additional 90,000 people are estimated to have been expelled from their homes this year. Further, the conditions under which campaigning took place made a mockery of free elections. The Serbian and Croatian leaders allowed no freedom of the media in the areas they controlled. In Sarajevo, Muslim leader Alia Izetbegovic prevented the launching of an independent, multi-ethnic television service.

Opposition leaders in all three communities suffered intimidation. Haris Silajdzic, the former Muslim prime minister, attempting to build a multi-ethnic party, was beaten up by members of the Muslim nationalist SDA. Freedom of movement was severely curtailed. Members of ethnic groups found outside their allotted areas were often threatened by truncheon-wielding police or sectarian gangs. There was no telephone communication across the ethnic boundary.

Ethnic cleansing was complemented by 'electoral cleansing'. Serbs who fled from Muslim-Croat areas to the Bosnian Serb republic were forbidden to return. Bosnian Serb officials bribed displaced Serbs living in non-Serb areas with aid and houses if they registered in the Serb republic. Some 240,000 Serbs took up the option.

Of the 400,000 displaced Muslims registered to vote in Serb areas, only 20,000 crossed the ethnic frontier. At least seven Serb mayors vowed to stop them. Indeed, the municipal elections were postponed until next year because of widespread evidence of nationalist rigging of voter registration. Hence, though voting was intended to be according to area of residence, in reality it took place overwhelmingly along ethnic lines.

The elections were intended to create shared multi-ethnic institutions that would begin to knit a divided Bosnia together again. But the principal leaders of the three communities campaigned on narrow nationalist platforms. They either openly called for secession or put forward policies whose logic is separation. An exception was Haris Silajdzic, who won only 14 percent of the Muslim vote.

Hardline nationalists swept the board. Izetbegovic was elected chairman of the joint presidency with 630,000 votes, compared to 508,000 votes for Krajisnik, the separatist Serb candidate. The Serb vote was split, however, with a moderate nationalist candidate, Ivanic, polling 242,000 votes. Izetbegovic won more than 80 percent of the Muslim vote, Zubak 88 percent of the Croat vote and Krajisnik 67 percent of the Serb vote.

But further evidence of rigging came from the turnout figures: 98.5 per-cent for the Serbs, 103 percent for the Muslims!

It is clear that the West—in particular the US—is trying to cover up the widespread incidence of fraud illustrated by these figures. As one UN analyst put it, the numbers voting are so inflated that 'it's as if nobody died at all throughout the entire war'. The elections were steamrollered by the US government, desperate to withdraw its troops in time for November's presidential election. Clearly, therefore, the polls have less to do with creating a permanent peace than with pro-viding Clinton with a foreign policy feather in his electoral cap. How-ever, they have merely served to legitimise ethnic cleansing and to consolidate the partition of Bosnia.

Chapter 18

Defying the dictators

Charlie Kimber

Recent events in Serbia and Croatia have finally demolished the myths which were used to justify Western intervention in the former Yugoslavia. They were myths that were swallowed by many on the left, and led some socialists to support armed action by their own ruling class.

The first myth was that there was no prospect of revolt by ordinary people against the regimes in former Yugoslavia, and therefore the only hope for those suffering so terribly was to call on the UN or some other outside agency. Some versions of this theory claimed that all Serbs were united behind their leaders' nationalist expansionism. Others suggested there was dissension but the weak opposition did not have the strength to challenge a cruel and ruthless government.

Yet for many weeks, beginning on 18 November, Serbia's president Milosevic was powerless to halt daily mass demonstrations in all his country's major cities. The protests had been sparked by Milosevic's decision to annul election results which had shown his party losing out in 15 of Serbia's 18 biggest towns. Western journalists commented on the fact that Milosevic did not send police and soldiers to crush the marches and speculated on whether this was a sign of his liberalisation. In fact it was evidence that Milosevic feared the revolt would spread from the streets to the heart of the state forces.

The street protests were not led by left wingers. The most conspicuous spokesman of the Zajedno (Together) coalition which headed the demonstrations was Vuk Draskovic. Although he now sometimes poses as a liberal, Draskovic is basically a Serbian nationalist who

First published January 1997

came to prominence by specialising in rabble rousing speeches against 'Bolsheviks' and 'Communists'. He was one of the main leaders of the 1991 protests against Milosevic in Belgrade. Already known as the 'King of the Squares' for his ability to whip up a crowd, Draskovic led a series of big marches which almost toppled the regime. The fear that he would be driven from power was one of the main reasons why Milosevic racked up his nationalist baiting in 1991. He was successful because he played on two weaknesses in Draskovic's politics—his nationalism and his refusal to focus on workers and strikes.

In 1991 Milosevic was weak in many respects, but he was quite capable of taking on all comers in a contest to see who could be the most vocal and vicious Serbian nationalist. But despite the leadership it is clear that the recent protests have also involved very many people who share nothing of Draskovic's politics.

A journalist who has recently returned from Serbia said, 'Several students I spoke to said they hated Draskovic and thought the Zajedno leaders were little better than Milosevic. But who else was standing up for change? If there had been some other force calling for revolt, it could have grown quite quickly. Draskovic rests on middle class support, not the mass of people.'

This journalist also reports two other important factors:

> A group of about 30 metal workers from a factory near Belgrade who were on strike about unpaid wages came to one of the demonstrations. They were hesitating whether to join the march when some of the Zajedno people started shouting at them, 'Get back to work. We will build Serbia through hard work.' Of course they left. I asked people why they had not protested about Milosevic before. It was not because they were scared, but because before they had felt Serbia was under pressure from outside forces and everyone had to stick together. I got the real impression this revolt would have come two years earlier if Milosevic had not been able to point to the sanctions, the NATO air strikes, the US troops and so on.

Far from destabilising the Serbian regime which the West professed to detest, it is now clear that intervention has helped to prop it up. Even now, although the US had backed the opposition movements, British ambassador Ivor Roberts has tried desperately to broker a deal to save Milosevic. According to the *Daily Telegraph*, Roberts' endeavours on behalf of British commercial interests with the Serbian regime has earned him the nickname 'Ratko' Roberts, a reference to

General Ratko Mladic, the Bosnian Serb military leader.

While Milosevic was battling to stem the tide of revolt, his counterpart in Croatia, Franjo Tudjman, was also facing marches and strikes. Again the immediate issue was electoral fraud but, as in Serbia, what lay behind this was disenchantment with the promises made during the war and the continuing desperate poverty.

Over 100,000 marched in Zagreb in December and rail strikes shut down much of the freight service for over a week. Strikes were threatened in several other areas of industry and among transport workers. 'We have had enough of the dictatorship. We have had enough of being told our enemies are abroad when we cannot even have a free press at home,' one protester told reporters.

Tudjman heads one of the most right wing governments in Europe. Yet he was feted by the West and many on the left during the war. He was used as the sword to slay the Serbian dragon and backed up by waves of NATO air strikes. The Krajina invasion, the most brutal piece of ethnic cleansing of the whole war, was carried out by Tudjman's forces with the full backing of the US.

With every day that passes it becomes more obvious that the Dayton peace agreement has solved none of the region's basic problems. Over a year since the deal was rammed through by US pressure ethnic cleansing has not been reversed, refugees remain wrenched from their homes and three repressive one-party states have been fixed in office. It is these regimes, central to the whole Dayton process, which are now being fought in the streets of Zagreb and Belgrade. If reports at the end of December are to be believed, we can soon expect more protests in the streets of Sarajevo against the Bosnian Muslim regime as well.

Socialist Review argued throughout the war in the former Yugoslavia that however difficult it might be to conceive it happening, the only future was for workers to unite across boundaries and ethnic divisions and that Western intervention would be disastrous. Both elements have now been proved correct.

The London conference which recently reviewed Dayton offered no prospect of improvements for the mass of people, no end to the 50 percent unemployment, the spiralling inflation or the luxury lives of the rich while the majority suffer. Instead it simply rubberstamped plans for the 31,000 troops in the multinational force to take over from 20 December in the SFOR 'stabilisation force'. The real hope in the region is for the protests we have already seen to grow and develop, and in particular to connect with workers' demands and genuine socialist politics.

Chapter 19

Arising from the ashes

Andreja Zivkovic

The heroic victory of the mass democratic movement in Serbia, which has forced dictatorial president Slobodan Milosevic to recognise the results of November's local elections, represents the first real blow for democracy in the region. It is also the first breach in the reactionary 'Pax Americana' imposed on the people of the former Yugoslavia at Dayton, Ohio, in December 1995.

The Dayton peace agreement was faithful to previous Western peace plans in recognising and legitimising results of mass ethnic cleansing and genocide. Behind the official rhetoric of a united, multi-ethnic Bosnia, its *de facto* partition into three ethnic statelets was being sanctioned. The policing of this iniquitous 'new order' fell largely to the dictators of the region—Milosevic, Tudjman and Izetbegovic—whose one-party regimes were now cemented by Western support. By challenging Milosevic the protesters in Serbia have also confronted a Western *realpolitik* founded on the dominant powers of the region. As an editorial in the *New York Times* noted, US foreign policy for the region has been thrown into utter confusion by Milosevic's capitulation to popular protests, since it is no longer sure that he can hold the line in Bosnia.

This process was by no means accidental. It was Milosevic's new role (made in the US) as 'strongman of the Balkans' and the delusions of grandeur it fostered that led him to overplay his hand. And recent events in Croatia suggested that the West would tolerate almost any attack on democracy just so long as the regional status quo was properly maintained. Tudjman refused to accept the defeat of his party in the capital, Zagreb, in local elections in September 1995, and imposed

First published March 1997

135

his own mayor on the city. Neither this, nor the repression of any independent media, nor one of the worst human rights records in Europe prevented Croatia from being admitted to the Council of Europe. This encouraged Milosevic to believe he could safely ignore Western protests while riding out domestic opposition. However, when protests involving hundreds of thousands exploded in all the major Serbian cities, the West was forced to criticise Milosevic, and broke off a commercial agreement favourable to Serbia. This breathtakingly cynical posturing on the part of the West could not prevent the beginning of the end for the post-Dayton New World Order in the Balkans. And Milosevic was left floundering around in utter bewilderment in the face of the forces he had unleashed.

During the war Western imposed sanctions meant Milosevic was able to blame the West for the dire economic straits of workers and thus to enforce 'national unity'. However, beneath the apparent stability of the regime the war itself was slowly dissolving the chains that bound workers to their leaders. As sanctions produced mass unemployment, and as the ensuing hyper-inflation forced the majority of people into destitution, the masses began to tire not only of the war but also of the sirens of nationalism. The ever flexible Milosevic responded by shifting from 'Greater Serbia' nationalism to a pro-peace stance. In this he was aided by a nationalist political opposition that had previously tried unsuccessfully to outbid him in national chauvinism, and which now attacked Dayton as a betrayal of the Serbian nation. Hence Milosevic's trouncing of the opposition in the federal elections of 3 November. By now sick of nationalism, the people supported Dayton, an end to the war and the lifting of sanctions. This translated itself into a vote for Milosevic.

The local elections reflected the other side of the coin. Here the people punished the corruption and self enrichment of the ruling party-state bureaucracy. Radicalised by a war that has seen a minority become fabulously wealthy while the majority starves, most people were no longer so prepared to accept the status quo. So when Milosevic decided to annul local election results all the accumulated bitterness at mass unemployment, pauperisation, political repression and state control of the media suddenly exploded into mass rebellion.

At first the movement was largely composed of students and the urban middle classes since the workers, reduced to apathy and despair by effects of hyper-inflation and mass unemployment on their living standards, remained atomised and marginalised. But the rising movement gave confidence to those who were laid off (on state benefits) to join the marches. Those at work were threatened with the sack if they were not at work on demonstration days. And where the workers threatened to take matters into their own hands, as in the seething industrial centres of Kragujevac and Nis, the regime immediately conceded the opposition election victories or paid back salaries owed—which was enough to satisfy the movement. Workers were not willing to sacrifice all merely to put into the saddle an opposition whose lust for power and weak commitment to democracy are well known, and whose pro-market strategy promises further misery and unemployment. Consequently Milosevic was able to demobilise industrial workers by playing on these fears and defending the social policies of the Titoist system.

So workers, while probably making up the majority of the marchers, did not impose their class demands and methods on the movement. And so the protests remained dominated by an opposition which was able to impose its strategy— of boycotting parliament and lobbying the West to put pressure on Milosevic—largely unchallenged. Hence, despite protests mobilising up to half a million people, the movement was unable to achieve the critical mass necessary to overthrow the regime.

In addition, the opposition refused to open the black pages of the nationalist past to critical discussion and limited its demands to those— recognition of election results, liberalisation of the media—that would catapult it into power. Refusing to demand real democratic changes meant blunting the revolutionary edge of the movement. Under these conditions Milosevic could sufficiently recover his political composure to pursue a carrot and stick strategy that has limited victory to a reinstatement of the local election results.

But if the combined exertions of Milosevic and the opposition have so far stifled the potential for a 1989-style revolution they have not been able to prevent the protests from turning into a festival of the oppressed. In the carnival atmosphere of mass demonstrations in cities like Belgrade, ordinary people are liberating themselves from their previous state of servile dependence on, and fear of, the regime which has lost forever its ability to command the automatic respect and fear of the people. Thus a new period is opening in which, as one student leader puts it, 'nothing will be the same again'. The potential for further radicalisation is most clearly expressed among students. A whole generation is becoming politicised.

Milosevic could not prevent the example of the movement from spreading across national frontiers and divisions of the Balkans to

Bulgaria and Albania. In Bulgaria, opposition to the catastrophic social effects of Socialist Party mismanagement of the economy was largely inspired by the mass street protests in Belgrade. And in turn the opposition protests emboldened workers to launch national strikes and to reject a government that many previously had looked to for protection against the worst ravages of the transition to a free market. A national education strike was organised in Serbia at the beginning of February in protest at the annulment of election results, and workers in the largest engineering factory in Serbia threatened to go on strike. The fact that Milosevic's decision to retreat suspiciously coincided with these actions suggests that he probably feared that they would escalate into a general strike.

The democratic spirit raging across the Balkans clearly demonstrates that whatever the local origins of protests, there is a tendency for them to generalise as economic struggles feed into political challenges to existing regimes, and vice versa, as political struggles cause people to challenge their chronic economic situation. This is clearest in the case of Bulgaria and Albania where, respectively, economic collapse and casino capitalism are leading to rejection of incompetent, corrupt and authoritarian regimes. In Serbia the protests are primarily political in origin. They are also fuelled by a situation in which the mass of people have been thrown into destitution by the war and confront a tiny, corrupt elite.

However, in the absence of real socialist leadership the protests are likely to remain limited, fragmented and ideologically confused and thus open to manipulation or even repression. In Albania the lack of any leadership has meant that the protests have quickly descended into directionless riots which may leave people defenceless in the face of state repression. In Bulgaria the very success of the movement has created its own problems. Whoever wins the forthcoming elections will collude with the IMF to impose a vicious austerity and shock therapy programme to force the economy to follow the dictates of the market. The cost will, as usual, be borne solely by workers.

Workers in Bulgaria have so far not really come to terms with the abysmal future that beckons, as can be seen from one of their recent slogans: 'We are here not because of ideology, but because of our stomachs—too much hunger.'

In Serbia the movement faces, to differing degrees, a combination of repression by the ruling class and the prospect of a painful transition to the market. The opposition, in refusing to call a general strike and in calling off protests for a free media until 9 March, is allowing a deeply split ruling class time to recuperate. Transfixed by the prospect of parliamentary and presidential elections, Zajedno is leaving the movement without any real focus or strategic direction. But genuine mass struggles cannot be switched on and off at will like a tap. Unless they move forward rapidly and generalise, they are likely to dissipate.

In destroying Milosevic's aura of invincibility the mass protests have blasted open a new chapter in Serbian politics, namely that of Milosevic's decline. This is not to say that he is doomed to defeat, but rather that he will never regain his absolute authority and that for the moment his star is on the wane. In this context he will certainly be tempted to unleash a spiral of violence from which, given the refusal of the opposition to mobilise the working class, he can only benefit. This might take the form of engineering a new crisis in Kosovo to divert popular anger into anti-Albanian pogroms, followed by the declaration of a national state of emergency. And without a class critique of nationalism even the most war weary people can be led by the nose by a 'national saviour' on horseback.

More optimistically, the spring has awakened a critical spirit amongst the people, creating the very real potential of new struggles in the not too distant future. Furthermore the movement has lit a beacon that offers hope and guidance to others in the region. As in the case of Bulgaria and Albania, struggles that originate in response to local issues can be radicalised by the example of other, quite different, movements. This can initiate a transnational process of mutual conditioning and dialogue, in which the learning curve of class struggle spirals from economic to political questions and back again. Then workers and the oppressed may once more come to unite across the barbed wire ethnic frontiers in the teeth of attempts by their respective ruling classes to divide them. This is the key to progress in the region.

As the crisis deepens the alternatives facing the region polarise: either the use of populist nationalism and state coercion, war or terror, by the 'left' or right, to impose the transition to the free market, or a socialist alternative based on a class alternative to the region's national conflicts and economic problems.

Chapter 20

Shooting stars

Chris Harman

The street scenes could have been those of 1989. Huge demonstrations day after day. Not just in one country, but three simultaneously. Continual speculation about whether governments would fall or order troops to open fire and therefore risk civil war.

That was the picture in the southern belt of Eastern Europe last month. In Bulgaria, Albania and Serbia the pattern was very similar, and in each people told journalists they were inspired by the protests in the neighbouring states.

Yet, superficially, the issues behind the protests seemed very different to each other. In Serbia demonstrators saw themselves as fighting the unfinished business of 1989—marching behind liberal and nationalist politicians against the rigging of elections by a ruling party in its fifty second year in power.

By contrast, in Bulgaria the issues were not primarily political but economic—a combination of slump and inflation that had driven the mass of people to near destitution. The government was in the hands of the successor party to the old Stalinists, and the anti-Communist opposition called for its removal. But it was a government that had emerged from 'free' elections, after a spell with the opposition in power and still controlling the presidency.

In Albania the issues were a mixture of the economic and the political, of the Bulgarian and Serbian factors. The pyramid based investment funds into which a sixth of the population had put their life savings collapsed and huge numbers of people were pushed into desperate poverty overnight.

President Berisha's government, generally believed to have rigged last May's elections, was closely identified with those who ran the funds, and tried to use armed police to drive protesters from the streets, leading to bitter fighting and near insurrection in parts of the country.

First published March 1997

But there was one glaring difference with both Serbia and Bulgaria. Berisha's Democratic Party is not descended from the old Stalinists, but took office after they were driven from power in 1990 by the only sustained general strike anywhere in Eastern Europe. Berisha modelled himself on Margaret Thatcher and appeared on the platform alongside her at the 1991 British Tory party conference. And, until very recently, Western bodies treated Albania as one of the star economies of Eastern Europe, claiming its massive privatisation programme had led to an 'economic miracle' with one of the highest growth rates in the world.

But the growth rates were inseparable from the pyramid funds, and these were bound to collapse. They work along the same lines as chain letters. People are persuaded to subscribe by the promise of huge interest rates, which are paid out of the subscriptions of those who join later. Sooner or later new people stop joining and there is no money left to pay back what most subscribers have paid in.

The scam is one of the oldest in the history of capitalism, and enjoyed a much publicised vogue—and collapse—in Romania, Russia and Serbia. At the same time Albania under Berisha was meant to be experiencing an economic miracle. In reality, Berisha was using the scam to bolster his position while relying on the same police and secret police who had kept Enver Hoxha's Stalinists in power for half a century to establish a one-party state of his own.

There is a simple reason the various Western bodies failed to see this. Free market economists had a very simple explanation when the economies of Eastern Europe went into tailspin in 1989-90—it was all the fault of state intervention in the economies. Once this was removed through extensive privatisation and deregulation, rapid economic growth would follow. They were bewitched by the 'miracle' in Albania because it seemed to prove how right they were.

In fact the collapse of the miracle into conditions barely different to those in Serbia and Bulgaria should cast doubt on all their arguments, and on the conventional wisdom of much of the left as well as the right.

In *Socialist Worker* and *Socialist Review* we insisted in the late 1980s that you could only fully understand the upheavals throughout the old Eastern bloc if you broke with the conventional wisdom. What we were witnessing was not the failure of socialism, but of a particular stage in the development of capitalism—state capitalism.

This had arisen in the inter-war years, leading to the belief that state intervention could prevent capitalism ever again experiencing devastating crises.

The eruptions of crises in both the West and the East in the 1970s and 1980s dealt a blow to these beliefs. Many of the former enthusiasts for state intervention now reverted to the free market views that had prevailed until the 1930s—ignoring the prolonged crisis of those years and claiming that 'freeing markets' would lead to rapid economic expansion.

We insisted, by contrast, that neither continued state capitalism nor 'reforms' in the direction of market capitalism could overcome repeated crises. Such crises, we predicted, would force the state capitalists to embrace market mechanisms but then, in turn, to resort to further lunges in the direction of state intervention in a futile attempt to ward off instability. What is more, governments, whatever their 'democratic' rhetoric, would attempt authoritarian measures—and would face resistance from workers and students who still remembered the upheavals of 1989. But such resistance could only be partially successful until a new generation of workers' leaders emerged who understood that the official 'socialists' did not stand for socialism, nor the official 'democrats' for democracy. The danger, as in 1989, was that it would be derailed by 'round table' compromises with governments rather than by fighting for a completely different sort of society.

The coming together of the crises in Serbia, Bulgaria and Albania bears out our arguments.

Chapter 21

Albania: beyond the fragments

Dave Beecham

Order is being restored in Tirana—for the world's press at least. But whatever the outcome of the uprising, one thing is certain. The order being restored will not satisfy the Albanian people.

The scale and violence of the March uprising caught everyone by surprise, yet it should not have. A people which was promised freedom from oppression and a chance to enrich itself has been reduced to beggary by a corrupt, authoritarian regime.

Capitalism as a system depends on credit—a term derived from the Latin word *credere*, to believe. Like many before them, the Albanian people believed the promises and then were swindled out of all they had. When the EU poured in $500 million in aid and created a phoney boom, Albanians believed that at last they had a chance of a better life. They have been portrayed as simple and naive, but it is only a couple of years since Western governments and their advisers were portraying the country as a glowing example of capitalist liberalisation.

The Albanians' belief was no different from that of those people in the US in the Reagan years who put billions of dollars into deregulated savings and loans (building society) schemes only to discover they were riddled with fraud. The only real difference between what happened in Albania and the US lies in the fact that the US state could bail out the savings and loans schemes and avert the bankruptcy of the nation.

The media experts and politicians alike throw up their hands in horror at the 'chaos' of the Albanian uprising. But the uprising was itself a reaction to the chaos wrought in people's lives, the betrayal of hopes, the broken dreams. The people's reasonable response was to protest, to seek compensation, and to demand the removal of the man they saw

First published April 1997

as principally responsible. When Sali Berisha unleashed the army and the secret police, the people again responded in the most intelligent way. They persuaded the soldiers to join them, raided the barracks, broke open the armouries, took over their towns and villages, and seized stocks of food.

This was not chaos—it was, potentially, the birth of a new order. It was an amazingly peaceful process, considering the years of repression. The only real venom was directed at Berisha and his henchmen, and the secret police, the Shik. Yet even they were mainly spared the summary execution they deserved.

The misfortune of the Albanians is that an uprising demands a leadership worthy of the people. In some areas this has happened, above all in the south of the country. Mass meetings have elected town and village committees which have won widespread local support, preventing looting and organising transport, food distribution and medical supplies. But an uprising is like a vast chemical process: the scum can also rise to the top. There are gangsters on both sides, seeking to take advantage of the situation. Berisha's new militia has been recruited from the underworld, while in Vlorë, for example, the rebellion appeared to include speculators with links to organised crime in Italy. Local drug barons also seem to have been involved.

At the same time figures from the old Stalinist regime appear everywhere. Berisha is, of course, a former member of the apparatus, who subsequently shed his skin and slithered over to promote an Albanian version of Thatcherism in the Democratic Party (PSDS). The newly appointed prime minister, Fatos Nano, was a reform economist under the old regime of Ramiz Alia and is now leader of the Socialist Party (PSS)—the former Stalinist party under a new name. During the uprising Alia was sprung from jail, where he was serving a nine year sentence for abuse of power, and is now no doubt negotiating for a return to the 'government of national stability' which he led in coalition with the PSDS in 1991-92.

At local level some Socialist Party cadres clearly have popular support: the PSS has a particularly strong base in the countryside. Yet the most striking thing is that throughout most of Albania the appeals of the party leaders had little or no effect on the uprising. The people do not trust the professional politicians, which makes the determination of the EU governments to support them with police 'advisers' even more dangerous than their usual adventures in the Balkans.

But the EU and the US cannot stop interfering in the Balkans, even if some governments are much less enthusiastic than others. Albania is not a backwater like Rwanda, where the slaughter only becomes really embarrassing to the Great Powers when it reaches the level of genocide. Albania matters.

The instability of the southern Balkans, stretching from Durrës in the west to Istanbul in the east, is the historic faultline of imperialism. It was here that the old Ottoman Empire broke up, first with the creation of Serbia, Bulgaria and Romania in 1878, and finally with the expansion of the Austro-Hungarian Empire, the creation of Albania, and the expansion of Serbia, Greece and Bulgaria on the eve of the First World War. The aftermath of that war saw huge transfers of population—the term 'ethnic cleansing' had not yet polluted the language—alongside the creation of Yugoslavia and the consolidation of the Greeks in Macedonia. The big loser was Turkey. The big winners were Serbia and Greece, acting under the protection of the Great Powers, France and Britain, whose main preoccupation at the time was to seize control of the Middle East, which they achieved in 1920.

For the Balkans the legacy of this period of butchery and intrigue—and the horrors which followed the Italian and German invasions during the Second World War—was a patchwork of ethnic groups and national minorities, each suffering discrimination and most mistrusting each other. As a result the region is beset with conflicting territorial claims.

Albania did not exist until 1912. Historically its roots are in Kosovo, 90 percent Albanian but controlled by Serbia. In neighbouring Macedonia, formerly part of Yugoslavia, 20 percent of the population is Albanian. Macedonia's newly won independence is hardly recognised by Greece and Bulgaria, which both claim parts of the country. To the north, in Bulgaria, there is a large oppressed minority of Macedonians and, alongside them, a Turkish population which has suffered continued religious and political persecution by the authorities. Meanwhile, back in Albania, there is a Greek population which is concentrated in the extreme south of the country—right in the heart of the current revolt.

Karl Marx once wrote that the past weighs like a nightmare on the minds of the living. Nowhere is this more obvious than in the southern Balkans. On top of the imperial legacy is the Stalinist one: in particular the repression of Kosovo and the Bulgarian minorities. In both cases the regimes have used the national question and the 'threat' of a breakaway to help divert popular anger away from the authorities. As the different

Balkan states grapple with continuing economic crisis and mass unemployment, the potential exists for such diversions on a far wider scale.

For both the EU and the US governments, the nightmare scenario is a conflict which brings in the two NATO members Greece and Turkey, the historic rivals for control, still at loggerheads over Cyprus. Both Greece and Turkey have been armed to the teeth in recent years, mostly with NATO tanks and planes, as the other NATO powers have scaled down their forces. The interests of the Great Powers, as ever, lie in a balancing act—divide and rule—to prevent a strong regional power emerging.

For socialists, the history of the Balkans is both an object lesson in the terrible legacies of imperialism and Stalinism, and an important test. The rights of national minorities have to be defended—but there are no national solutions. Any attempts by outside powers to 'resolve' the issues will, as in the past, intensify the conflicts. Socialists have always argued that the only way out of the cycle of economic crisis and national conflict in the Balkans lies in social revolution and a federation of independent states.

The Albanian uprising may seem doomed to be diverted into banditry or, worse, some nationalist adventure. Yet beneath the surface there are other forces at work. The symbolic salute of those involved in the uprising was not the two fingered 'V for Victory' of Berisha's party, nor the raised fist of the old regime. It was three fingers: the thumb and first two fingers of the right hand. That is not an Albanian salute. It is traditionally a Serbian one. It was the salute seen night after night on the television in the closing months of last year—the salute of those demonstrating in Belgrade against their hated president, Milosevic.

One gesture does not make a revolution. But it is a symbol of the power of people to generalise, to make connections between their own struggles and the struggles of those they might in other times consider their enemies. Just as workers in Western Europe can link arms in the struggle against Renault, those in the Balkans have shown that internationalism is not an empty slogan.

Chapter 22

Another fine mess

Judith Orr

A year after the mass anti-government protests in the Serbian capital, Belgrade, the streets are once again filled with demonstrators. Last year they were protesting at Slobodan Milosevic's attempts to deny opposition parties seats won in the municipal elections, which saw him lose 15 of Serbia's biggest towns, including Belgrade. Now they are protesting about the removal from office of Zoran Djindjic, Belgrade's mayor, who was one of the most popular of last year's opposition leaders. In a show of power Milosevic then sent in police to smash up the demonstrations and took back an independent television channel which since last year had been a challenge to the state run media.

Last year's marches were hailed as the 'Velvet Revolution' which saw rare unity between opposition leaders and hopes raised of an alternative to Milosevic's nationalism. But the leadership was more interested in doing deals and powerbroking. Rather than develop into a serious movement of organised workers, the movement remained as popular street protest and the price is being paid today.

The recent election saw Milosevic lose control of the Serbian parliament, and Zoran Lific, Milosevic's candidate for president, lose to the far right nationalist Vojislav Seselj, leader of the Serbian Radical Party. Although this election has to be rerun because the turnout was below the required 50 percent, the result has sent shockwaves throughout the area. Milosevic was forced to give up the post himself in the summer as he had served for the two term limit. But he planned to maintain control by taking up Lilic's old job, the largely ceremonial presidency of federal Yugoslavia, and turn it into a role with real power, while he used Lilic to promote his interests. The lack of any effective alternative challenging Milosevic from the left has left the door open for those further to the right to appear as if they offer a solution to the ordinary people of Serbia.

First published November 1997

The elections in neighbouring Bosnia have been equally messy. On the one side both the Serbian Radical Party and Milosevic are backing the faction led by Radovan Karadzic—still wanted for war crimes—and Momcilo Krajisnik. On the other is Biljana Plavsic, the Bosnian Serb republic's president, who accepts the Dayton peace accords and is, as a result, the preferred candidate of the West. Such is the Western governments' support for Plavsic that during the election the NATO peacekeeping forces actually captured a television and radio transmitter that was broadcasting anti-Plavsic propaganda and handed it over to her.

How the election results will be upheld remains to be seen. Displaced refugees had the right to vote in elections in towns in which they were a majority before the ethnic cleansing of the war. As a result it appears that the displaced populations may have won victories in towns currently run by other ethnic groups. For instance the Serbs who now control Srebrenica have lost the election there to Muslims, but there is no obvious mechanism to put this election result into practice. However, not all election results reflected nationalistic division. Candidates advocating multi-ethnic tolerance won in Tuzla.

But the problems thrown up by the elections are the obvious result of the peace agreement that was imposed by the West. The Dayton accords left the nationalism that broke up the former Yugoslavia enshrined in a patchwork map in which there is still no agreement even on such apparently superficial issues such as the design of a Bosnian flag. The election of candidates who fundamentally reject the whole agreement and the carefully drawn borders show up the faultlines and the contradictions and are a further illustration that Western intervention only exacerbates the problems in the region. As a result a lasting solution in the Balkans, where people are offered a real alternative to the dangerous squabbling of their leaders, is still a long way off.

Chapter 23

Europe's apartheid

Sabby Sagall

A week long offensive early in March by Serbian police against armed guerrillas of the Kosovo Liberation Army (KLA) in the Drenica area near the Kosovan capital, Pristina, resulted in the massacre of at least 80 ethnic Albanians (who are largely Muslim and make up 90 percent of the population). The official justification for the Serbian action was the heightened level of terrorist activity by the KLA against Serbs in the previously autonomous province of Serbia. But many Albanians claim that the onslaught was also directed against the civilian population as a method of intimidation, and of choking off support for the KLA.

The causes of the conflict lie deeper. It was in 1989 that Serbian president Milosevic (today president of rump Yugoslavia) launched his campaign of virulent nationalism with the claim that the Kosovan Serbs (10 percent of the Kosovan population) were under threat from Albanian nationalists. Milosevic revoked the autonomy which had entitled Kosovans to run their own affairs in areas such as education, health and social policy. His chauvinism drew an echo from the leaderships of the other national republics, sparking the vicious civil war which led to the break up of Yugoslavia.

In 1989 the Serbian authorities carried out a purge of Albanians from public and professional life. They closed down the Albanian language university and secondary schools. They sacked almost every Albanian doctor and nurse, replacing them with Serbs. But for over eight years Albanians have resisted this form of apartheid by building a network of parallel institutions. Factories, garages, restaurants and even private homes became schools, clinics and administrative offices. Under pressure Albanian students are only now being allowed back into state schools, but this has in turn provoked mass protests from Serb nationalists.

At the end of 1995 a small group of Kosovan militants lost patience

First published April 1998

with the pacifist strategy of the Democratic League of Kosovo, led by Ibrahim Rugova. Targets have included Serbian traffic police and Albanians professing loyalty to the Serbian state. The KLA began seriously arming itself last year. Close ties of family and clan solidarity link Albanians in Kosovo, Albania and Macedonia. The Serbian police onslaught can only intensify support for the KLA.

Meanwhile, Western governments are once again worried that the struggle in Kosovo could spill over into a Balkans wide conflict, engulfing Macedonia and possibly Greece and Turkey. Members of the Contact Group (US, Russia, Britain, France, Germany and Italy) have threatened intensified sanctions against Serbia unless the government withdraws its special police units. However, they are not prepared to back the demand for secession, calling on Serbia merely to restore the pre-1989 autonomy status. Clearly, the Western ruling classes bear a major share of the blame for the chaos of Yugoslavia. They are an integral part of the problem and cannot be part of the solution. An *International Herald Tribune* report from Serbia indicates that, in contrast to the early 1990s when Milosevic whipped Serbs into a frenzy of war, he is now so unpopular that it is more difficult for him to play the nationalist card. Only working people in the various independent republics have the potential to overcome their national divisions and create an alternative to the chauvinist nightmare of politicians such as Milosevic.

Chapter 24

The West's blind eye

Kevin Ovenden

The human toll from Serbian president Slobodan Milosevic's offensive in the province of Kosovo is appalling. Nearly a quarter of a million people have been driven out of their homes. Over 40,000 have crossed the border south to Albania. Serbian police, army and paramilitary units stormed into Kosovo in February to crush the separatist fighters of the Kosovo Liberation Army (KLA). About 90 percent of Kosovo's population of two million are Albanian and their support for independence from Serbia has grown since 1989 when Milosevic removed the province's autonomy and began a systematic campaign of repression. Over the last six months the Serbian forces have adopted a scorched earth policy, moving from village to village, scattering the inhabitants. The KLA, which only two months ago controlled large areas of central Kosovo, was in full flight by the end of August. And from the Western leaders, who between 1992 and 1995 told us that Milosevic and the Serbs were the sole source of the war in Bosnia, comes scarcely a word.

The reason is plain. Behind the bluster about 'Serb atrocities', Western governments have been working to ensure that the KLA is weakened and fails to win independence for Kosovo. Clinton, Blair and Kohl may not be ecstatic that the Serb army has overrun all of Kosovo, but they are enormously relieved that the KLA does not have the upper hand. Fred Abrahams from Human Rights Watch describes the attitude of Western diplomats in Kosovo: 'They are telling journalists that the West has turned a blind eye to Serb abuses in order to force the KLA to the negotiating table.'

They did more than turn a blind eye. The Swiss government cooperated with the US to freeze millions of dollars in KLA bank accounts

First published September 1998

in July. The German government said it would follow suit. Every Western government said it opposed independence for Kosovo and denounced the KLA as 'terrorists'.

The Great Powers want to preserve the existing carve up in the Balkans. US diplomat Richard Holbrooke says in his new book, *To End a War*, that the Dayton peace agreement which he negotiated deliberately avoided mention of Kosovo. Western governments fear that independence for Kosovo will call the division of the Balkans into question. It could lead the Albanian minority in neighbouring Macedonia, for example, to demand independence. That in turn could lead to border disputes between Bulgaria, Greece and Albania.

Other states oppose the KLA for even more direct reasons. Turkey, a member of NATO, has tried to maintain influence in the Balkans since the collapse of the Ottoman Empire in 1923 by claiming to be the protector of the Albanian Muslim minorities there. But the Turkish government rounded on the KLA. If Kosovo was entitled to independence from an oppressive state, then why not the oppressed Kurdish minority in south east Turkey?

So the KLA, which called for NATO intervention against Serbia, was left to fight alone. Despite sabre rattling from US Secretary of State Madeleine Albright, Pentagon officials told journalists last month, 'We need to tell the KLA that the cavalry is not coming.'

In fact, US and NATO forces are already intervening heavily in the Balkans. They have a military presence—20,000 troops in Bosnia, and forces in Macedonia and Albania engaged in 'military exercises'. CIA agents kidnapped two Islamic activists in June in the Albanian capital, Tirana, with Albanian government help. They have a diplomatic presence, with US diplomats frantically trying to prevent a dispute over the stationing of anti-aircraft missiles in Southern Cyprus in November from spilling over into conflict between Greece and Turkey.

The tragedy of Kosovo is a product of decades of big power intervention and support for rival, blood soaked nationalisms in south east Europe. That will only end when workers and peasants break from their rulers and reject the nationalist poison.

Letter from a Serbian student

The economy is collapsing, inflation is growing, there is low pay and unemployment. But somehow we are surviving.

The situation in Kosovo is also quite shitty. The television and mass media are giving very little information and telling lies. But we know what is happening. People are not in a really nationalistic mood. A lot of Serbian people and workers do not hate the Albanians and feel a little sympathy for them. But mostly people are afraid of another war—80 percent of all new soldiers are sent to Kosovo. A lot of my friends are there and no one is older than 21. People don't want another war. Some independent organisations have organised activities and distributed leaflets against the war. I'm absolutely against the war and I will not go to Kosovo to shoot poor Albanians.

In 1974 Kosovo became the seventh republic in the Yugoslav federation. And then the hatred started. Some Albanians who had wanted to break away from Yugoslavia started to work on it. The police began to terrorise them but the Albanians started to terrorise Serbs, so a lot of Serbs ran away from Kosovo.

I'm not talking about all Albanians. The genocide that took place— if we can call it that—was carried out by Albanian extremists and it was an answer to the police genocide against Albanians. This lasted for over ten years and then Yugoslavia split up and the Montenegrin bourgeoisie started real terror against the Albanians and they are now fighting for their freedom.

In the last few months there were some signs of moves towards autonomy in the regions of Vojvodina and Sumadija-Pomoravge. I support this, but not totally because we are maybe more far from revolution, but maybe it would be good to decentralise Belgrade's absolute power.

The only solution of all problems in Yugoslavia and everywhere is the revolution of all the exploited, terrorised, tortured and there will be no more wars, hatred, exploitation. Revolution is the only solution, the only way out.

A lot of young soldiers have died in Kosovo and I'm really sorry and angry at the same time. All of those boys are 18, 19 or 20 years old. I am 19 and if I didn't pass my faculty entrance exam I would be sent to Kosovo. It is very bad what the police are doing to the Albanians. There are a lot of examples of Albanian villages where all the people are buried. It is really bad.

Chapter 25

The carve up continues

Clare Fermont

Our leaders and media have once again been whipping up support for bombing raids in the Balkans—this time ostensibly to save the people of Kosovo from the Serbian army. With massacres being shown on our televisions almost daily and up to a quarter of a million Kosovan refugees starving on hillsides, it was argued that doing *something* must be better than doing nothing. But the truth is that the *something* being demanded is not better than nothing. It is worse.

What would happen if there were air strikes? Even a few raids would result in many civilian casualties, of both Serbs and Kosovan Albanians, and the deaths of reluctant young Serbian conscripts. The idea of bloodless strikes using so called 'smart' bombs and cruise missiles was well and truly exposed during the bombing raids of Iraq during the Gulf War. All commentators agree that limited air strikes would not remove Serbian forces from Kosovo. So the attacks would have to be much more sustained, leading to massive destruction, huge numbers of casualties, and the threat of all out war with Yugoslavia—disaster on an unimaginable scale.

But let us imagine that air strikes were somehow quickly 'successful'. What would that mean for Kosovan Albanians? According to the military and political objectives spelt out by the US and its NATO allies, the refugees would be able to return to a devastated land still dominated by the very Serbian forces that terrorised them into flight in the first place.

The truth is that it does matter who is in charge of the proposed raids and what their motives are. NATO is the military alliance of Western imperialism led by the US. Among its revered members is Turkey,

First published November 1998

whose oppression of Kurds is every bit as horrific as that of Serbia towards ethnic Albanians. NATO is not driven by humanitarianism. If it was, its planes would long ago have bombed Turkish military bases to free the Kurds in south east Turkey.

So what does drive NATO policy in Kosovo? Certainly not sympathy with the long Kosovan battle for independence. Of the two million Kosovans, 90 percent are ethnic Albanians, who speak a different language to Serbs, have a separate culture and are mainly of a different religion. In 1974 Kosovo's limited autonomy within the former Yugoslavia was extended to match that of other republics—with the crucial exception that Kosovo was denied the constitutional right to secede. In the early 1980s mass demonstrations by ethnic Albanians calling for Kosovo to be made a full republic were violently crushed. In 1989 Serbian president Milosevic removed Kosovo's autonomy altogether, reducing it to an administrative region of Serbia, and immediately suppressed the Albanian language and cultural institutions.

In 1990 Serbia dissolved Kosovo's government. The next year, following a secret referendum, ethnic Albanian leaders proclaimed an independent 'Republic of Kosova' and set up a parallel state. This was declared illegal by Serbia and suppressed. Every day Serb police harassed, imprisoned and tortured ethnic Albanians.

With all peaceful and democratic routes closed to them or met by violence, Kosovans turned to the armed struggle, organised from 1996 in the Kosovo Liberation Army (KLA). Despite a pathetic lack of arms, its mass popular support and persistent attacks on Serb forces meant the KLA was a real threat to Milosevic's government of Yugoslavia (which now comprises Serbia, including Kosovo, and Montenegro). By February this year the KLA controlled significant areas of Kosovo.

In all these years the NATO allies have consistently ignored the plight and resistance of Kosovans. The 1995 Dayton agreement that carved up the former Yugoslavia and signalled the end of the worst fighting in Bosnia explicitly excluded Kosovo. When desperate ethnic Albanians were forced to take up arms to defend themselves in Kosovo, NATO leaders condemned the KLA as evil terrorists and in effect gave the green light to Milosevic's counter-insurgency operations.

So long as Milosevic was containing the Kosovan struggle, none of the NATO leaders cared. When Milosevic sent in troops earlier this year to crush the KLA, NATO did nothing. It was happy to see the KLA weakened. Massacres did not suddenly begin this summer. On 5 March, for example, 54 ethnic Albanians were butchered in the village of Donji Prekaz near Srbica.

All this was ignored by NATO because it feared that success for the Kosovan independence movement could spark similar demands by Albanians in neighbouring Macedonia, which could lead to Albania, Bulgaria, Greece and Serbia becoming embroiled in wars about territory over which all have claims. NATO allies only responded when the scale of the atrocities became so great that refugees started pouring out of the country, threatening to create a very unstable situation. That fear of instability in the region is the key to NATO's policy.

The Western rulers need Milosevic. They need him to sustain the carve up of the Balkans drawn up at Dayton, which sealed the triumph of hardline nationalism. Alongside Milosevic and his extreme nationalist deputy in Serbia, the ultra-nationalist Franjo Tudjman remains in power in Croatia. Recent elections in the Croat and Serb parts of Bosnia have brought extreme nationalists to power. Any serious weakening of Milosevic by Western bombs could open the door for renewed nationalist land grabbing by such leaders and throw the whole region back into chaos.

If Western leaders were truly concerned about the Kosovans they would have used the billions of dollars spent on military intervention on the displaced Kosovans; they would have opened their doors to the refugees who reached their borders; and they would have supported Kosovan independence. They have done none of these things.

Instead, they play increasingly dangerous war games. The US and its allies are eager to prove that they are the world's policemen. But their military needs can conflict with their political needs, which demand that the national boundaries they have drawn up around the world remain intact.

Tony Blair and Robin Cook tell us that their warmongering has produced a deal which will benefit everyone in the Balkans. The truth is exactly the opposite. In Yugoslavia the effect of the threats has allowed Milosevic to clamp down on all opposition. Two independent radio stations and three newspapers that were critical of his government have been closed down. The threat of attack by US imperialism has bolstered nationalism. As a result, the left inside the country is more isolated. Eighteen months ago mass demonstrations against Milosevic almost toppled him. Since then there have been many signs of opposition, including by workers. A day after the air strikes were called off, a demonstration against Milosevic in Belgrade attracted only a handful of people.

In Kosovo the ethnic Albanians can either stay in their makeshift shelters on freezing hillsides or go back to burned out villages and place their faith in 2,000 unarmed monitors who are supposed to guarantee their safety against heavily armed Serb police and soldiers.

There is no guarantee that the disaster of NATO military attacks will still not take place. In the meantime, the chief effect of the deal brokered under the threat of such attacks has been to weaken the two forces most likely to improve life for people in the region—the Yugoslavian working class and the Kosovan independence movement.

Chapter 26

The resistible rise of Slobodan Milosevic

Andreja Zivkovic

War returned to the Balkans in the 1990s because of the massive economic and political crisis that rocked Yugoslavia in the 1980s. Faced with a rising arc of workers' resistance, the rulers of the different republics unleashed a terrifying wave of nationalism to force through market reforms and to hold on to power. In 1987 Milosevic was the first to use nationalist scapegoating in his campaign against the Kosovans, who he accused of genocide against the Serb minority in Kosovo. He soon found willing imitators in the other republican rulers, who blamed the crisis on the federal government and urged increasingly separatist solutions to their own nations' problems. It was this logic of nationalist inflation that was to eventually destroy Yugoslavia. However, it was a close run thing, with nationalism and the politics of all-Yugoslav class struggle vying for the allegiance of the different nations.

Even as workers capitulated to the sirens of nationalism, they continued to pursue their autonomous class aims. Unable to completely dupe the workers, and traumatised by the worker and student rebellion of March 1991, Milosevic was forced to launch a murderous war.

As he embarked on a dummy invasion of Slovenia, around 80 percent of Serbs supported the 'preservation of peace by any means', with 23 percent refusing to fight in a war that they did not believe was theirs. The West now intervened to defend the integrity of the federation in the noble cause of ensuring the repayment of Yugoslavia's

First published May 1999

debt, effectively backing Milosevic. When the war spread to Croatia, this position was undermined by Germany's unilateral recognition of Croatian independence, under a regime which not only refused to grant its Serb minority real national rights, but which was actively engaged in its persecution. This tragic and cynical intervention enabled Milosevic to claim the mantle of saviour of the Croatian Serbs as well as to use them as a battering ram against the right to self determination of the Croatian people.

Despite the mood of war hysteria cultivated by the regime, workers' nationalism was basically defensive. Workers in their thousands expressed mute opposition to the war in the form of draft dodging and desertion from the front. However, Western imposed sanctions from 1992 enabled Milosevic to blame the West for the dire economic straits in which workers found themselves. Around 500,000 young people, the backbone of the anti-war and democratic movement, emigrated. Loyalty to Milosevic's Socialist Party (SPS) was ensured through doling out favours to party cadres who ran the most important concerns in Serbia as well as the sanctions busting franchise, thus creating a tiny stratum of millionaires overnight. To integrate those sectors of the ruling class who depended on state protection to maintain their privileged status a substitute 'radical socialist party', the United Yugoslav Left (JUL), was formed under the leadership of Milosevic's wife, Mirjana Markovic. However, this corrupt and unstable regime could only survive through a system of constant purges of suspect institutions and terror against its opponents. The paramilitary police was reinforced to act as Milosevic's personal guard against the army and to discourage dissent, and the media pumped out disinformation.

To cater for workers disillusioned by corruption, mass unemployment and the plunder of state property, Milosevic created both the 'radical leftist' (JUL) and proto-fascist (Serb Radical Party) parties in the early 1990s. Led by the demagogue Vojislav Seselj, the latter was used to create a puppet opposition which concentrated on discrediting any real opposition movements. Access to certain social benefits was made conditional on membership of the corporatist, SPS led trade unions. The key enemy here was NEZAVISNOST, the independent trade union federation which not only opposed the regime but also demanded an end to the war and a democratic settlement to the national question in the former Yugoslavia. Beneath the apparent stability of the regime the war itself was slowly dissolving the chains that bound workers to their leaders. As sanctions produced mass unemployment, and as the ensuing hyper-inflation forced the majority of people into destitution, the masses began to tire not only of the war, but also of nationalism. From 1993 onwards Milosevic was forced to drop 'Greater Serbia' nationalism and sue for peace to keep in step with the popular mood.

At the end of 1995 the West came to Milosevic's aid once more. Conceived in order to stabilise the region, the Dayton peace agreement recognised and legitimised the results of mass ethnic cleansing and genocide. Behind the official rhetoric of a united, multi-ethnic Bosnia, its *de facto* partition into three ethnic statelets was being sanctioned. The policing of this new order fell largely to the dictators of the region (Milosevic, Tudjman and Izetbegovic), whose one-party regimes were now cemented by Western support. Milosevic could now claim that a vote for his party was a vote for peace. So when elections to the federal parliament came at the end of 1996, the SPS and its allies benefited from a popular desire for peace to trounce the non-opposition that only knew one tune, 'Greater Serbia' nationalism. But in local elections the people punished the corruption, self enrichment and authoritarianism of the party regime by voting for the opposition coalition, Zajedno. No longer intimidated into silence by the war, and radicalised by its privations, wide layers of the working class had begun to break with the SPS. When Milosevic refused to recognise the election results all the accumulated bitterness suddenly exploded into mass rebellion. For three months the cities of Serbia were taken over, day after day, by a mass democratic movement that mobilised hundreds of thousands. The regime was forced to concede victory to the opposition in order to prevent revolution in Serbia.

However, in victory lay the seeds of defeat and of the present war. For Milosevic owed his survival to an opposition which limited its demands to recognition of election results. By refusing to demand real democratic changes—purging of the state apparatus, destruction of the party-state machine, the prosecution of Milosevic and his clique as war criminals—Zajedno blunted the revolutionary edge of the movement. For a while, though, the regime's very survival was in the balance as workers threatened to take centre stage. Tragically, the self imposed limitation of the movement to the question of elections cut short the collective mobilisation of the working class against the regime. For who would risk all to put into the saddle an opposition notorious for its lust for power and weak commitment to democracy?

Nevertheless, in this period all the demands of striking workers were immediately met and opposition victories recognised in the seething industrial centres of Serbia. Indeed, it was fear of worker revolt which forced Milosevic to back down as a national education strike threatened to escalate into a general strike at the end of February 1997.

Writing in *Socialist Review* at the time, I warned that Zajedno's electoralist strategy could only lead to 'disarming the people in the face of the ruling class counter-offensive that will surely come at some point in the near future', and that in order to regain his authority Milosevic would 'be tempted to unleash a spiral of violence from which he can only benefit. This might take the form of engineering a new crisis in Kosovo to divert popular anger into anti-Albanian pogroms, followed by the declaration of a national state of emergency.' This has unfortunately come to pass. While the movement petered out into a fragmentation of demands, a regime on the brink of collapse was saved by an opposition that was imploding as its leaders fought over who was to become mayor of Belgrade. The West now intervened in the shape of British foreign secretary Malcolm Rifkind, who persuaded Milosevic to bring the opposition into government in return for the promise of Western investment. Bolstered by Western support, Milosevic hit upon the tactic of dividing the opposition, absorbing its main component, the SPO (Serbian Renewal Movement), into a 'government of national unity' that also included Seselj's fascists. Bereft of any principles and hungry for power, the SPO took the bait and its leader, Vuk Draskovic, was given the quite irrelevant position of deputy premier of Yugoslavia. Having destroyed the opposition Milosevic could now use the lifting of the trade embargo to demobilise an increasingly restive working class.

However, he still presided over a bankrupt, impoverished and truncated Yugoslavia with no apparent future and so latched onto increasing KLA resistance to police repression in Kosovo from the spring of 1998 to launch a military campaign against the Kosovans. The counter-offensive now began in earnest. First the students and lecturers, the most rebellious section of the mass movement, were neutralised by a law allowing the regime to directly appoint university rectors and faculty boards and forcing lecturers to sign humiliating new contracts as a sign of loyalty to the regime. Around 100 were sacked for refusing to do so, and a two month general strike by students against the law and for the reinstatement of the lecturers petered out in February 1999, leaving lecturers divided and students feeling betrayed. In October 1998 an information law was passed allowing Milosevic to crush the independent media. He was now able to reassert control over the party and state apparatus.

However, the regime was increasingly riven by vicious faction fighting. Key figures in the ruling class openly criticised Milosevic's strategy in Kosovo, fearing that it would lead to a further spell of international isolation for Serbia. The economic and political system was imploding at an alarming rate with only the glue of the Kosovo campaign to hold it together.

By the time of Rambouillet in February 1999, the West had decided to impose a settlement on Milosevic, one which firmly rejected the right of the Kosovans to self determination but one which also cut the 'strongman of the Balkans' down to size. The sting in the tail was the deployment of NATO troops to patrol the agreement, something that Milosevic could only accept at the price of political suicide. From then on war was inevitable.

On the eve of war most Serbs were resigned to the loss of Kosovo and were unresponsive to the war mood being whipped up from above. An attempt by nationalists in Belgrade to mobilise people to defend Kosovo failed miserably, with only a few dozen turning up to march. NATO's bombs have allowed Milosevic to present Serbia as a victim of a plot by the international community. As the real opponents of the regime have testified, Western bombs have undermined the fruits of a decade of anti-war, anti-nationalist and democratic opposition to the regime. Milosevic has been able to smash the last vestiges of the independent media in Serbia as well as silence any form of opposition with the assassination of the independent publisher, Slavko Curuvija.

We cannot predict how the war will end. At present, the West has neither the will nor the political unity to return the Kosovans to their homeland. More likely is a compromise deal followed by the partition of Kosovo. Sections of the ruling class and the army may well conclude that Milosevic must pay the price for this adventure. The army will almost certainly not accept another humiliation after its ignominious withdrawals from Slovenia, Croatia and Bosnia. Vojislav Seselj will certainly cry betrayal and might instigate a coup. But if Milosevic survives it will be the beginning of the end.

A post-war Yugoslavia will find itself in the grip of economic collapse and hyper-inflation, its people reduced to starvation, its political system imploding under the weight of bloodletting within the ruling class. The bombs will for a time silence workers for whom unemployment is directly caused by the West. Whether workers are able to impose a class solution to the crisis or succumb to Vojislav Seselj's fascist programme of national renaissance, or are simply crushed by Milosevic, depends on the politics of the movement.

History will be merciless to those who are unable to free themselves from the nationalist past and develop a new socialist understanding of their problems.

Chapter 27

Divide and conquer

Chris Harman

'The bourgeoisie of each country is...asserting that it is out to defeat the enemy, not for plunder and the seizure of territory, but for the liberation of all other peoples except its own.' Quotations from Lenin can appear like biblical texts, presented as sacred truths at the beginning of a holy sermon. But this one, written as the horror of the First World War was casting its bloody shadow across Europe, is relevant today, when NATO politicians tell us this is the first 'humanitarian war' and many who claim to be on the left concur.

Supposed concern for the horror being inflicted on small nations was central to the war propaganda of all the contending powers in the First World War. The catalyst for the war was Russia's reaction to the invasion of a small Slav nation, Serbia, by a large Germanic empire, Austria: 'Liberation of Serbia' was the Tsarist slogan. France's entry into the war was justified in terms of the opportunity to free the inhabitants of Alsace-Lorraine from the 'oppression' they had suffered at German hands since the annexation of the region after the Franco-Prussian War of 1870. Britain's pretext was the German occupation of 'poor little Belgium'. Germany's excuses for the war included the oppression of Poland at the hands of Russia—which led the most influential Polish nationalists to back Germany and to set up a puppet government on its behalf.

'Humanitarian' interventions did not end with the First World War. Hitler justified his intervention against Czechoslovakia in 1938 by talking not of German imperialism's drive for profits, but of the national oppression suffered by the German speaking minorities in the border regions of Bohemia and Moravia. Similarly, when the US

First published May 1999

stepped up its war in Vietnam in the mid-1960s, it claimed it was to protect those like the million Catholics who had chosen to move to the South when the country was divided in 1954.

What attitude should socialists have to calls for self determination in such circumstances? The starting point has to rest on two fundamental tenets. First, no group of oppressed people anywhere in the world can achieve their self emancipation unless they are able to decide on their own futures; the idea of one people forcing another to be free is a contradiction in terms. Second, the workers of one country cannot achieve their freedom if they continue to collaborate with their own rulers in oppressing the people of another country; as Marx put it, 'A nation which oppresses another cannot itself be free.'

These general principles have, however, to be applied in concrete circumstances that are often complicated by other factors. The most important are the drive of imperial powers to grab control of as much of the earth as possible, and the coexistence within the same geographic areas of different national identities putting forward contradictory national demands.

Imperialist wars almost invariably involve the Great Powers trying to use national movements against their opponents for their own ends. In some cases this amounts simply to providing a few weapons to movements which retain their own independence and follow their own goals—as with the attempts of the Kaiser's Germany to help the Irish uprising in 1916 or the help the Vietnamese struggle received from Russia and China in the late 1960s. But in other cases the once independent national movements have become mere playthings of imperialist powers. This was true, for instance, of the Slovak and Croatian governments established by Germany from 1939-45, or of the Polish government set up in German occupied Warsaw during the First World War. For socialists to support national movements that have acquiesced in such a role would be to help strengthen imperialism.

This was the issue Lenin and other revolutionaries had to confront. When the war began, he was quick to insist that Austria's suppression of Serbian national rights in no way justified lining up with Russia's 'war of liberation': 'The national element in the Austro-Serbian war is an entirely secondary consideration and does not affect the general imperialist character of the war.'

The whole international socialist movement had traditionally identified with the demand of the Poles for national rights. But once the Polish nationalists aligned themselves with the Kaiser, Lenin insisted:

To favour a European war purely and simply in order to obtain the restoration of Poland would be nationalism of the worst sort. It would place the interests of a few Poles above the interests of the hundreds of millions of people who would suffer in such a war…[for Polish revolutionary socialists] to put forward the slogan of Polish independence now, in the present relations which exist between Poland's great imperialist neighbours, would be to chase after a will-o'-the-wisp, to get lost in the pettiest form of nationalism.

When Russian liberals began to demand the freedom of Poland from German occupation, he reiterated, 'Russian Social Democrats must expose the deception of the people by Tsarism, now that the slogans of "peace without annexations" and "independence for Poland" are being played up by Russia, for in the present situation both these slogans express and justify the desire to continue the war. We must say, No war over Poland.'

The other complication, the coexistence of different national groupings with contradictory demands, has long been a feature of the Balkans. Capitalism developed late there and led to the middle classes from different linguistic groups (Serbs, Bulgarian and Macedonian Slavs, Romanians, Greeks, Albanians) each attempting to hegemonise the economic opportunities available in particular regions by drawing the peasants behind their own national banners. But each was too weak to do more than create a patchwork of territories which overlapped patchworks of territories influenced by their rivals. The fight for influence became the fight to expand rival patchworks into rival states, each with its own national mythology of a 'heroic past' going back many centuries, its own 'glorious' national monuments, national heroes—and its monopoly of well paid posts for those with the right national background. In each case, the other side of the establishment of the national state was the oppression of national minorities within it—Hungarians and Roma in Romania, Turks in Bulgaria, Serbs in Austrian-run pre First World War Bosnia, Slovaks and Roma in post First World War Hungary, Muslims in Greece, Greeks in Albania. In each case, too, the only way one weak national state could maintain its control over the minorities within its boundaries in the face of other weak states, which allegedly stood for the rights of those minorities, was to form close alliances with the major imperialist powers. Hence the history of the Balkans has been the history of Great Power interventions.

The nationalist mythology of Balkan peoples has repeatedly found enthusiasts among the European intelligentsia: Byron died fighting for the Greeks; Tolstoy's *Anna Karenina* ends with the hero going off to fight for the Serbs; fascists and left wingers alike enthused for Croatia in 1992. But the reality has always been very different from the mythology. Strengthening one 'national' Balkan state against its rivals has usually involved driving out, through the most barbaric means, groups which might identify with rival Balkan states. What is now called 'ethnic cleansing' was a feature on all sides in the two Balkan Wars of 1912-13, of the Turkish-Greek war of the early 1920s (with one million refugees on either side), of the Second World War (when Ustashe Croats butchered Serbs, Serbian Chetniks wreaked vengeance on Croats, and some Kosovan Albanians joined the SS, while Tito's partisans fought desperately to unite all ethnic groups against the German occupation). And, of course, it was a feature of the Yugoslav wars of the early 1990s, when not only did Serbs murder Muslims and Croats, but Croats waged a bloody murder campaign against Muslims in the Vitez and Mostar areas and 'ethnically cleansed' Krajina of its Serbian inhabitants, and Muslims slaughtered Serbs in the suburbs of Sarajevo. West European left wingers who started off by cheering on the 'national struggle' of Croats or Muslims ended up apologists for such actions, just as did those who cheered on the Serbian state. As Trotsky, who covered the horrors of the 1912-13 Balkan Wars as a journalist, observed 'for the benefit of nationalist romantics', 'Even in the backward Balkans...there is room for national policy only in so far as this coincides with an imperialist policy.'

How do these considerations apply to the present situation in Serbia and Kosovo? The imperialist purpose behind NATO's continuing war is clear. Even proponents of US imperialism like Kissinger who were hesitant about the need for war on 24 March are now convinced it has to be fought to the finish. They can see clearly the war has nothing to do with humanitarianism, but is about the insistence by US imperialism that it can punish any state that defies it. The war is completely at one with US policy elsewhere in the world.

Not so clear to some people is what has been happening to the Kosovan Albanian national movement. This grew in the 1960s out of the resentment of the Albanian majority in the region that they were denied the full national rights available to Slovenes, Croats, Montenegrins, Macedonians and Serbs. The Albanians were as much second class citizens in Kosovo as the Catholics in Northern Ireland or the Kurds in Turkey, although they had not always been the underdogs. The movement grew further when, after equal rights were briefly granted in the 1970s, these were taken away by Milosevic in 1989.

For the first half of the 1990s the movement took the form of passive resistance to the Serbian state. People accepted this policy because they realised they were too weak to win in direct physical confrontation. But after the failure of the Dayton agreement in the mid-1990s to take Kosovan Albanian rights into account, there was growing support for the approach of armed groups like the Kosovo Liberation Army.

Yet these groups also saw they were too weak to win if they took on the Yugoslav army by themselves. They therefore followed a strategy of seeking support both from nationalist groups inside Albania and among the Albanian minority in Macedonia. They also looked increasingly to drawing the US and other Western powers into the conflict by provoking Yugoslav retaliation against Kosovan Albanian civilians. Their tactics included attacks not only on Serbian police and Yugoslav soldiers, but also on Kosovan Serb civilians (bombs in cafes, the kidnapping of ethnic Serb miners and so on). The strongly pro Kosovan Albanian *Guardian* journalist Jonathan Steele reported last year that in some villages not only were Serbs ethnically cleansing Albanians, but the KLA was ethnically cleansing Serbs. This was the old logic of Balkan nationalism.

If the NATO forces give them some control in Kosovo, sections of the KLA will follow the same logic in the areas of Western Macedonia they claim for a Greater Albania. Such is the ethnic mix of Western Macedonia that they could not achieve their aims without the sort of ethnic cleansing the proponents of a Greater Serbia attempted in parts of Croatia and Bosnia. In the process they would also create a situation where other powers with claims on Macedonia (Bulgaria and Greece) or even on Serbia (Hungary and Bulgaria) would be tempted to intervene, with even more ethnic cleansing.

Under such circumstances there can be no excuse for any genuine socialist backing the KLA's nationalism. To do so would be to line up with an ally of imperialism and a proponent of ethnic cleansing, even if on a smaller scale at the moment than Milosevic's. Socialists certainly see a place for Kosovan self determination in a final, peaceful outcome for the region. It is difficult to see how Serbs and Albanians can ever live together peacefully unless they accept each other's rights, and this means Serbs accepting the right of Albanians to establish a state of their own in Kosovo if they so desire. But it also means the Albanians in

Kosovo and Macedonia guaranteeing to other ethnic groups, including the Serbs, their rights. Otherwise Kosovan self determination would simply mean the old Balkan game of one national group establishing a state, denying minority ethnic groups their rights, and leading to still more ethnic strife.

When early meetings of the Communist International discussed the Balkan Question they concluded that the only way to satisfy the different demands for national rights was in the context of a socialist federation of the whole region and not through the further proliferation of rival capitalist states, each entrapping embittered national minorities within them. But all these arguments are purely hypothetical while the NATO war against Yugoslavia continues, for it is reducing Kosovo and much of Serbia to one great bomb site, where national rights for anyone are a sick joke. Only if the war leads to revolutionary developments in countries like Greece will things be otherwise. Meanwhile, the responsibility of socialists in the bombing states is to do our utmost to bring the war to an end.

Chapter 28

New Labour, new war

Alex Callinicos

The Balkans have moved back to the place they occupied when this bloody century began, at the centre stage of world history. The military assault NATO launched against Serbia on 24 March looks set to develop into by far the biggest war Europe has seen since 1945.

This war was the result of miscalculation on the NATO leaders' part. Its pretext was the refusal by the Yugoslav president, Slobodan Milosevic, to accept the Rambouillet 'accords' on the future of Kosovo. A CIA coordinated report by the US intelligence community predicted in January what would happen if the West carried out its threat to attack in such circumstances: 'Milosevic doesn't want a war he can't win... After enough of a defence to sustain his honour and assuage his backers, he will quickly sue for peace' (*Guardian*, 19 April).

Bill Clinton and his advisers imagined that an attack on Serbia would be a rerun of the Anglo-American bombing campaign against Iraq which began just before Christmas—a television war which would cost no Western lives and make the president look good after the impeachment scandal. It is also evident that no serious thought was given to the possible consequences of bombing Serbia on Kosovo itself. As we now know Milosevic responded, not by surrendering, but by authorising the large scale expulsion of Kosovan Albanians. The bombing precipitated the humanitarian catastrophe that NATO leaders are now using to justify yet more bombing.

Why did Milosevic react in the way that he did? Contrary to the infantile attempts by NATO propagandists to demonise him as the new Hitler, Milosevic is the consummate opportunist, ready cynically to do just about anything to hang on to power. He saw off the last wave of

First published May 1999

mass opposition to his regime in 1996-97, in part by co-opting ultra-nationalists such as the monarchist Vuk Draskovic and the genuine fascist Vojislav Seselj.

Escalating the crisis in Kosovo may have been a way of keeping the nationalists onside. It may also have been politically impossible for him to accept the Rambouillet 'accords': most nation-states would find it hard to swallow Annex B, which would give NATO troops unlimited access to the whole of Yugoslavia—Serbia and Montenegro, as well as Kosovo itself. The mass expulsions are yet another tactic, as Misha Glenny, one of the best journalists to have covered the earlier bout of Balkan wars in 1991-95, explains: 'The refugees are part of the war (not a pre-ordained programme of ethnic cleansing); they are designed to sow chaos amid NATO but also to threaten the stability of the host countries' (*Observer*, 18 April).

Confronted with the appalling consequences of their actions, the NATO leaders now seem determined to escalate the war. The social democrats who hold office through much of the EU are trying to use their political capital as parties of the left to legitimise the assault on Serbia. Tony Blair has called it a war waged by 'a new generation of leaders in the United States and in Europe...who hail from the progressive side of politics... In this conflict we are fighting not for territory but for values' (*Newsweek*, 19 April). New Labour, new war.

In fact, as every serious ruling class commentator concedes, the war is being fought, not for democratic 'values', but because NATO cannot afford to lose. As the bombing began, David Buchan wrote in the *Financial Times* (26 March), 'The outcome will determine whether NATO, which now has "Partnerships for Peace" with 25 other non-allies stretching east beyond the Caucasus and the Caspian, will become—as it hopes—the predominant force for crisis management throughout Europe.'

One of the central thrusts of US foreign policy under Clinton has been to maintain and strengthen NATO. So the alliance has expanded into east-central Europe, where Poland, Hungary and the Czech Republic are now members. NATO's official doctrine now stresses the importance of 'out of area' operations, military action beyond NATO's borders. The ideology of 'humanitarian interventions' has emerged to justify these operations, despite the appalling history of such interventions in Lebanon, Somalia, Bosnia and Rwanda.

As for the big powers of Western Europe, the catastrophic failure of EU policy during the break up of Yugoslavia in the first half of the

1990s showed that they lack the unified political organisation and indeed the military resources even to maintain order on their own periphery. The French and British general staffs concluded last year that even their combined forces were too weak to win air supremacy over Serbia. So, for the EU as well as the US, NATO remains an indispensable instrument of state policy.

The credibility of NATO will be proved on the bodies of the Balkan peoples. Already the air campaign has widened into a comprehensive assault on the civilian infrastructure of Serbia. The Hungarian speaking area of Vojvodina has been cut off from the rest of Serbia by the bombing in what seems to be a criminally irresponsible attempt by NATO to stir up yet more ethnic tensions, with potentially dangerous consequences not just in Hungary but in the Hungarian speaking areas of Romania and Slovakia.

Journalists close to the Blair court claim that one of the main thrusts of the air assault is to bottle up the Serb forces in Kosovo and then to cut them to pieces with ground assault aircraft like the A-10 tank-busters and Apache helicopters. This is a recipe for wholesale carnage, in which many Kosovan civilians would perish alongside their Serbian persecutors. Meanwhile the *Observer* reports that NATO is planning for a 'semi-opposed' invasion of Kosovo by ground troops by the end of May, presumably after the Serbian army has been sufficiently softened up by air attacks.

Assuming that some such operation were mounted successfully, what would be the eventual outcome? A march on Belgrade seems inconceivable for both military and geopolitical reasons—it might lead to an irreparable break with both Russia and China, whose relations with the US are already deteriorating. In all likelihood Kosovo, or at least its southern rump, would become a wretched NATO protectorate confronting an embittered, impoverished Serbia ruled either by Milosevic or by someone worse like Seselj. And Serb and Albanian zealots would busily prepare for the next war.

This is an utterly appalling prospect. It indicates the complete bankruptcy and cynicism of NATO policy. More than that, the entire crisis over Kosovo underlines one fact above all others. In this supposedly 'post-colonial' epoch, imperialism is alive and well. The great military and economic powers are still bullying everyone else to obey their demands. The only sane response is to rally all the forces we can against this barbarous war—and, beyond that, against the system that makes such horrors possible.

Chapter 29

NATO and the new imperialism

John Rees

There are currently over 20 wars raging around the globe. So why was NATO so concerned with the one in the Balkans? The plight of the refugees was the stock pro-war answer. Yet there were 15.3 million refugees made homeless by war in 1995 alone. So why did the war in Kosovo, where US military might alone was 99 percent greater than the arms spending of the state it was fighting, command the attention of the world's great powers?

The causes of NATO's Balkan War cannot be found in the Balkans alone. Neither can they be found in the events of the few months before war broke out in March 1999. The origins of the war are much wider and go back much further than Serbia's relations with Kosovo. To see the whole picture we have to go back to the fundamental fact of European history at the end of the 20th century, the fall of the Stalinist states in 1989.

The end of these regimes, and German unification soon after, gave all the institutions of international capitalism an unrivalled opportunity to expand into Central and Eastern Europe. International capital began to 'cherry pick' those sites and markets which were most profitable. Investment quickly followed, which, though large in comparison to the capitals which made it, was not large enough to sustain a turnaround in most of the Eastern European economies. The European Community also talked of eastward expansion. But, in a Brussels bureaucracy which still regards Greek membership of the EU as a mistake because the economy is insufficiently prosperous, the integration of Eastern European states was always more of a carrot to encourage pro-market reform than an immediate policy goal. So it was that the

First published June 1999

fastest expansion into Eastern Europe came from NATO. 'NATO', reports the International Institute for Strategic Studies, 'has confidently extended its collective defence provisions to three new members of the former Warsaw Pact...while the EU's enlargement process remains mired in bickering over fundamental issues such as reform of the Common Agricultural Policy.'

Historians of the 1999 Balkan War will no doubt marvel that so little comment has been made about the fact that, in the very month that the war broke out, NATO integrated Poland, the Czech Republic and Hungary into the alliance. The southern flank of NATO between Hungary and Greece is now pierced by the states of the former Yugoslavia. This alone gives NATO a considerable strategic interest in controlling the Balkans. But there is more at stake. The effect of NATO enlargement is to swing the Iron Curtain to the east. Where once it used to divide Germany, it now runs down the eastern borders of Poland, the Czech Republic and Hungary. It ends at the borders of the former Yugoslavia. The next three states to be considered for NATO membership are a former republic of Yugoslavia itself, Slovenia, and Serbia's neighbours, Romania and Bulgaria. Thus the whole ten year long process of NATO's eastward push is now caught up with the fate of the Balkans in general and the former Yugoslav states in particular.

President Clinton expressed NATO's war aims clearly enough in an *International Herald Tribune* article in May 1999 where he insisted that 'lasting stability in the Balkans could only come if the EU and the US do for south eastern Europe what they did for Europe after the Second World War and for central Europe after the Cold War... We can do that by rebuilding struggling economies, encouraging trade and investment and helping the nations of the region to join NATO and the EU.' The nations of the area, Clinton continued, were already responding to the 'pull of integration' by sticking with their pro-market reforms and 'supporting NATO's campaign'.

The new Iron Curtain between Western and Eastern Europe is not the end of the Balkans' strategic importance for NATO. If we look along the southern flank of NATO, through Greece and Turkey, we see how closely the fate of this region is tied to another crucial area of post Cold War instability—the arc of oil states running up from the traditional spheres of Western interest in Iran and Iraq to the Caspian Sea and the newly independent states on Russia's southern rim.

Just as NATO expansion into Eastern Europe was being celebrated at the alliance's fiftieth birthday party in Washington a few weeks ago, another pro-NATO alliance was being constructed in the wings of that summit. At the Washington meeting Georgia, Ukraine, Azerbaijan and Moldova joined with Uzbekistan to form GUUAM, a new alliance aimed at strengthening the member states' economic and political ties with the West. Three of these states—Georgia, Uzbekistan and Azerbaijan—only pulled out of the Russian dominated Confederation of Independent States' collective security pact this spring. GUAAM has agreed low level military cooperation but claims it is not a military alliance aimed against Russia. But GUUAM's formation comes hot on the heels of the Ukrainian parliament's decision to rescind its previous order to get rid of nuclear weapons, a direct result of the Balkan War. And as plans for NATO ground forces in Kosovo were being drawn up, Azerbaijan offered to send troops as part of the Turkish batallion. The US, although not keen to directly intervene in the Caucasus, is however 'keen for Turkey to be its surrogate there', according to the *Economist*. And as the Balkan War has developed, the nations of the Caspian area have 'plainly divided into pro-Russian and pro-NATO camps'. A GUUAM 'peacekeeping batallion is now to be set up under NATO auspices'.

So it is not surprising to find Russia's foreign minister asking, 'How should we understand the fact that this new regional organisation has been created in Washington during a NATO summit?' An answer to this question was provided by Eduard Shevardnadze, president of Georgia, who said, 'When I met Javier Solana [NATO secretary-general] I asked him, "When will you finally admit Georgia to NATO?" He whispered in my ear, but I can't reveal what he told me.' In all likelihood what Solana told Shevardnadze was that NATO won't be signing Georgia up in the very near future. This is because the main significance of the GUUAM area for the Western powers is still more economic than military at the moment.

GUUAM's main task, according to the *Financial Times*, 'is to develop the area's rich oil and gas deposits to the exclusion of Russia'. To this end, 'aligning with GUUAM from the outside are Turkey, Britain and the US—nations that have proved far more able than Russia to invest in and trade with the region.' There is indeed a rich prize at stake in the Caspian Sea region. Its proven oil reserves are estimated at between 16 and 32 billion barrels, comparable to the US's reserves of 22 billion barrels and more than the North Sea's 17 billion barrels. Total reserves could be as high as 179 to 195 billion barrels according to the US Energy Information Administration. Chevron's Tengiz field is the largest oil reservoir discovered in the last 25 years and contains six billion barrels. A one billion barrel field is now considered to be a 'big, world class find', according to the *Financial Times*. The Offshore Kazakhstan International Operating Company (OKIOC), whose shareholders include Mobil, Total, Britain's BG, Statoil of Norway and the US's Philips corporation, is investigating a field in the north Caspian said to be three times the size of Tengiz. No wonder the *Financial Times* reports that 'the political implications of a discovery could be more far reaching than the potential commercial rewards. A big find would...be a big boost to US policy in the Caspian region.'

These reserves are all a long way from the Balkans, but the routes by which the oil must come west are not. In April a new pipeline was opened carrying Caspian Sea oil through Azerbaijan and Georgia. The oil will continue its journey by tanker through the Black Sea, the Bosporus and on past the Turkish and Greek coast. The *Financial Times* records that an oil find by OKIOC 'could support the construction of a big export pipeline such as the trans-Caspian link to Baku in Azerbaijan, and then on to Ceyhan on Turkey's Mediterranean coast. Such a pipeline is a US foreign policy priority, as it would help wean the former Soviet republics along the Caspian away from Russia while undermining growing commercial interests in using Iran as an oil export route.' Other possible western pipeline routes lie through the Ukraine, Bulgaria and Greece—which are, respectively, a GUUAM member, an aspiring member of NATO and an existing NATO member. And the *Economist* reports that NATO 'says it may advise the GUUAM club on security—especially for the pipelines'.

All these routes give the necessity of security in the Balkans an additional direct economic importance to add to the primary strategic concerns which stand behind NATO's war in the Balkans. As US energy secretary Bill Richardson explained last November:

> This is about America's energy security... It is also about preventing strategic inroads by those who don't share our values. We are trying to move these newly independent countries toward the West. We would like to see them reliant on Western commercial and political interests... We have made a substantial political investment in the Caspian and it is important that both the pipeline map and the politics come out right.

It is the 'pipeline map' to which Richardson refers that connects the Caspian Sea oil reserves to the security of the area between Turkey, Greece and the other Balkan states. There are, as the *International*

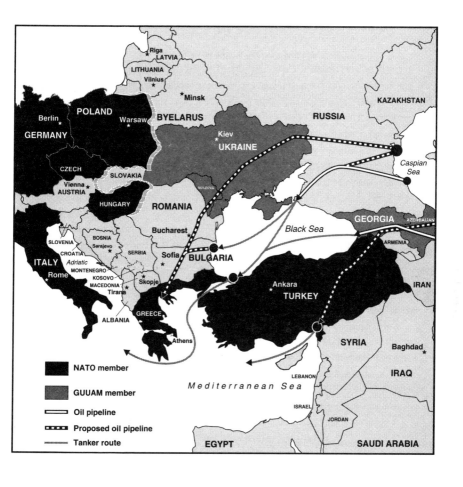

Herald Tribune points out, 'profound economic and geopolitical consequences' stemming from the decisions about the routes by which
the oil will come west:

> Rivalries played out here will have a decisive impact in shaping the
> post-Communist world, and in determining how much influence the
> United States will have over its development.

Geographical expansion is not the only way that NATO has altered
in the 1990s. It has now explicitly redefined its 'strategic concepts' so that
it is no longer simply a defensive alliance, as it claimed throughout the
Cold War. All the old Cold War NATO practices remain—including its
commitment to 'first use' of nuclear weapons if it deems such use to be
necessary. But immediately after the fall of the Stalinist states in 1991,
NATO redefined its aims so that 'out of area' operations became part of
a new 'strategic concept'. At first this was seen as primarily a 'peacekeeping' role. But, reports the International Institute for Strategic Studies, 'NATO's exclusive command of the Implementation Force (IFOR)
operations in Bosnia completely changed this view.' Thus the collapse
of the Eastern European regimes and NATO's expansionism fuelled its
concern with the Balkans; and its experience in the Balkans fuelled its
determination to use military weight beyond its borders. At the Washington Summit, a Combined Joint Task Force for rapid force deployment in 'areas of crisis' was grafted onto a revised NATO military
structure.

The results of these decade long trends are enormous. The Cold War
structure which underpinned the nuclear stalemate between the West
and the Eastern bloc has disappeared. This means that 'hot wars' are
no longer pushed to the colonial and former colonial periphery of the
system in the way that they were during the Cold War. These conflicts
continue, though they are fought less between national liberation
movements and colonial or neo-colonial regimes and more frequently
between politically independent states which can quickly move from
clients of the major powers to 'rogue' or 'terrorist' states if their interests
and those of the major powers diverge. Iran, Iraq and Serbia are just
the most prominent examples of the last ten years. This pattern is
going to continue, if only because 75 percent of US arms sales in the
past five years have been to countries whose citizens have no right to
choose their own government.

Even more importantly, the collapse of the Warsaw Pact has created
a zone of imperialist conflict stretching from NATO's new eastern

border through the Baltic states, Eastern Europe and the Balkans, through to the southern rim of Russia and the GUUAM states. This economically weak and unstable region is now a major zone of rival imperial claims. The Balkans have become a contested area once again because the tectonic plates of the major powers now grind against each other in this area, just as they did before the accident of Cold War imperial geography and the long postwar boom gave them temporary respite.

The New World Order promised ten years ago will not be delivered. The imbalance between US military power and that of every other state in the world, once touted as the guarantee of a more peaceful world, now stands exposed as a source of greater instability. US military spending is greater than all the military spending of the next 13 countries ranked beneath it. Yet the US share of world trade and world manufacturing is substantially less than it was during the Cold War. This is one central reason why military might is so often the policy of choice for the US ruling class. The other reason is the economic enfeeblement of Russia. But the policy of using this weakness to carry Russia reluctantly along with NATO objectives has its limits, as the course of the Balkan War so far shows. Moreover, as NATO encroachment comes ever closer to Russia's borders, the still enormous military machine of the Russian state may once again begin to look to the country's leaders like its one real asset in a threatening situation.

When we see the Balkan War in context it is no surprise to find that the 1990s have already been one of the bloodiest since the Second World War in terms of war deaths. Most of those killed have been civilians. Fifty years ago half of war deaths were civilian. In the 1960s civilians accounted for 63 percent of war deaths, in the 1980s that figure rose to 74 percent, and in the 1990s the figure is higher still. Only the destruction of the imperialist system will stop this carnage.

Chapter 30

Letter from Belgrade

'We are writing to you in these difficult moments of our shared suffering. Convoys of Albanians and other citizens of Kosovo, among whom were many of you, were forced to leave their homes. The killings and expulsions, homes destroyed and burnt, bridges, roads and industrial buildings demolished, paint a sombre and painful picture of Kosovo, Serbia and Montenegro, as in indicating that life together is no longer possible. We, however, believe that it is necessary and possible.

'The better future of citizens of Kosovo, Serbia and Montenegro, of Serbs and Albanians, as citizens of one state or closest neighbours, will not arrive by itself or overnight. But it is something we can and must work on together, as we have many times in the past, not so long ago. We know that it will now be very difficult and sometimes very painful. The example of the German-French post-war reconciliation and cooperation could serve as a model and stimulus.

'For the sake of future life together, the pain of crime has to be revealed so that it is, with forgiveness, remembered. This tragedy, yours and ours, personal and collective, is a result of a long series of erroneous policies of the most radical forces among us and in the international community. The continuation of these policies will take both Serbs and Albanians into the abyss. Also, the road of collective guilt is a road of frustration, continuation of hatred and endless vengeance.

'That is why this road has to be abandoned. Our first step of distancing from hatred, ethnic conflict and bloody retaliations is a public expression of our deepest compassion and sincere condemnation of everything that you and your fellow citizens are experiencing.

'As citizens of Serbia, we today suffer destruction and casualties as a result of NATO bombing, armed conflict in Kosovo and long lasting

First published June 1999

180

economic and social troubles under the burden of the dictatorship's deadly policies. Ethnic cleansing, NATO bombing and armed conflict should stop because they are not contributing to the solution of the Kosovo crisis but are only making it deepen. There should be no more casualties. All refugees should be allowed to return safely to their homes and live in the manner appropriate for free and proud people.

'We are convinced that together we will find strength and courage to step on the road of peace, democracy, respect of human rights, mutual reconciliation and respect. Dialogue, political negotiations and peace process have no alternative. For all of us, it is the only way out of the war conflict. It is the safest way to secure the return of refugees to their homes, to renew normal life and activities and find a solution to the status of Kosovo.

'In order to make this happen, we have to join our efforts to end the war conflict, revitalise the peace process and reconstruct, economically and democratically, the development of Kosovo, Serbia and the entire Balkan region. We are convinced that by joining forces we can contribute to the reaching of a just and rational political solution to the status of Kosovo, and build confidence and cooperation between Serbs and Albanians.'

Letter to Albanian friends signed by the following organisations: *Association of Citizens for Democracy, Social Justice and Support for Trade Unions, Belgrade Circle, Centre for Democracy and Free Elections, Centre for Transition to Democracy, Centre for Policy Studies, Civic Initiatives, EKO Centre, Belgrade Women Studies Centre, European Movement in Serbia, Forum for Ethnic Relations and Foundation for Peace and Crisis Management, Group 484, Helsinki Committee for Human Rights in Serbia, The Student Union of Yugoslavia, Union for Truth about Anti-Fascist Resistance, VIN—Weekly Video News, Women in Black, YU Lawyers' Committee for Human Rights, NEZAVISNOST Trade Union Confederation, Centre for Women's Studies.*

Index